Geography 2
BOOK 3

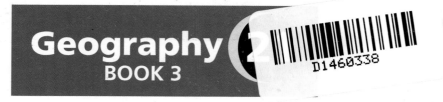

THE
WORLD

Published by Collins Educational
An imprint of HarperCollinsPublishers Ltd
77-85 Fulham Palace Road
London W6 8JB

The HarperCollins website is:
www.fireandwater.com

© HarperCollinsPublishers Ltd
First published 2000

ISBN 0 00 326696 6

British Library Cataloguing Data
A catalogue record for this book is available from the British Library.

Project management and editing by Susannah Baccardax
Internal design by Glynis Edwards
Page layouts by Janet McCallum/Wendi Watson
Cover design by Derek Lee
Illustration management by Susannah Baccardax/Wendi Watson
Illustrations by Cedric Knight, John Elsey, Belinda Evans, Jerry Fowler
Picture research by Charlotte Lippmann
Production by Kathryn Botterill
Printed and bound by Scotprint

Dedication

To Maggy and all who loved her

Acknowledgements

Jill and Ronald Russell
British Airways
Pat and Andrew Webb
Ann Hopkins
Charles Eaton
Elspeth Goat
Hazel Rymer
Population Concern
Save the Children
Stephen Golding
Marcela Leos Turpin of the Consulate of Mexico
Sally McIver of Toybox
Rachel Bader of Jubilee Action
Ross Wilson of Viva Network
Steve Brace and Ben Hartshorn of ActionAid
Damon Stanwell-Smith of Frontier
Laura Battlebury of the World Conservation Monitoring Centre
Friends of the Earth
CAFOD
OXFAM
WaterAid
Christian Aid
Vincent Bunce
National Cotton Council of America
Yosemite National Park

Acknowledgements Photographs

Every effort has been made to contact the holders of copyright material, but if any have been inadvertantly overlooked, the publishers will be pleased to make the necessary arrangements at the first opportunity.

ActionAid: 96 102 103 104 105 107
Andrew Testa/Panos Pictures: 43
Associated Press AP: 26
Bruce Coleman Ltd: 83
David Oswin: 50
Dokumentation: 41
Environmental Images: 30
Jubilee Action: 72t 73t 73b
National Cotton Council of America: 121 122
NHPA: 21b 23b 52t 58 60t 60b 63 64 78b 79 82 87 110b
Panos Pictures: 36 67 71m 92 110t
Popperfoto: 17 25 29 42 45 54
Robert Harding Picture Library: 17b 61t 61b 70b 71t 86 93 111t 111b 115 118t 125t 125b
S.O.A. Photo Agency: 118b
Science Photo Library: 34 48 56t 76 116
South American Pictures: 57m 68 74 75m 75b 84bl 84mr
Still Pictures: 99br 99t
Tony Stone Images: 6m
Woodfall Wild/ Lawson Wood: 78t
Woodfall Wild/ Nigel Hicks: 35
Woodfall Wild/Bob Gibbons: 52b
Woodfall Wild/David Woodfall: 6l
Woodfall Wild/Jeremy Moore: 6br
Woodfall Wild/Nigel Hicks: 31

Geography 21
BOOK 3

THE
WORLD

Simon Ross
Head of Geography, Berkhamsted Collegiate School

Series Consultant: Michael Raw
Head of Geography, Bradford Grammar School

Collins
Educational
An Imprint of HarperCollins*Publishers*

CONTENTS

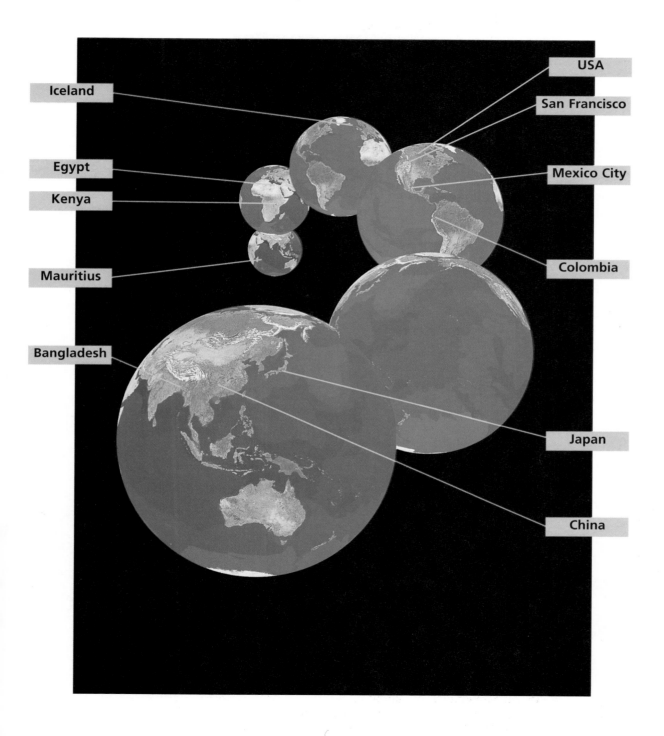

Iceland

USA

San Francisco

Egypt

Kenya

Mexico City

Mauritius

Colombia

Bangladesh

Japan

China

A global sense of place

How good is your geography of the world? Do you know which is the largest of the seven continents? Where to find the Indian Ocean? What the mountain range in South America is called? Throughout this book you will come across many maps of the world. It is important to take time to improve your basic global geography.

1 A geography of the world

The Earth is very special place. As far as we know, it is the only planet capable of supporting life. It is a planet offering a great many opportunities. The seas are teeming with life, the land can support forests and produce food for us to eat, and the air provides us with oxygen, without which we would not be able to survive.

1.1 The Earth has many resources ▶
which we can make use of

Population
Global population is 6 billion and is growing by 90 million people each year.

Rainforests
Over 130,000km² of rainforest is cut down every year.

War and refugees
Wars have resulted in many refugees. There are now over 20 million refugees living away from their homes.

Species
Hundreds of species of animals and birds are endangered and may become extinct.

Global warming
There is increasing evidence for global warming which may lead to rises in sea levels and changes in the climate.

Water
A quarter of the world's population does not have access to safe water.

1.2 Some threats to the survival of our planet

However, there are also threats to our planet, mostly as a result of our own actions. Look at Figure 1.2. Issues like wars, global warming and the destruction of rainforests may be a threat to the survival of our planet. These and other issues will be studied later in this book.

Look at Figure 1.3. It is a map produced by a Year 9 pupil describing 'Geography in the News'. It shows the locations of a selection of recent world events. Notice that some of these could be considered as 'threats' to the well-being of our planet.

1.3 Some recent world events

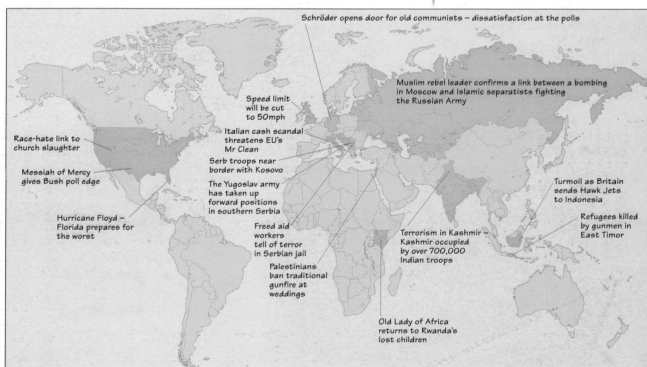

1 Look at the Photos in Figure 1.1.

a Work in pairs to list the opportunities offered by:
- the land
- the sea
- the air

b How do each of the issues in Figure 1.2 pose a potential threat to the well-being of our planet?

2 Study Figure 1.3.

a Work as a class to make your own list of some current or recent global events.

b Produce a labelled map, similar in style to Figure 1.3, plotting the location of the events you have identified. Use Atlas Maps A and B (pages 10–11 and 12–13) to help you. Use colours and possibly sketches or cut-out photos to illustrate your map.

The Physical World

Look at Atlas Map A on pages 10–11. It shows the continents of the world and some of the major physical features such as mountains and rivers.

Table 1.4 lists the seven continents in order of their size. Locate them all on Atlas Map A (pages 10–11). The continents make up about one third of the surface of the Earth. The rest is ocean. The Pacific Ocean, with an area of over 165 million km², is by far the largest ocean and is four times the size of the largest continent, Asia.

▼ *1.4 The continents in order of size*

Continent	Area (million km²)	Percentage of total land (%)	Degrees (°) on pie chart
Asia	43.6	29	104
Africa	30.3	20	
N. America	25.3	17	
S. America	17.6	12	
Antarctica	13.3	9	
Europe	10.5	7	
Oceania	8.9	6	
Total		100	360

3 For this activity you will need a blank outline map of the world. Use Atlas Map A on pages 10–11 to put in the following information. Use a pencil first, then use colours and ink for the labels.

a Mountain ranges:
- Himalaya Mts (Asia)
- Alps (Europe)
- Rocky Mts (North America)
- Andes (South America)

b Oceans:
- Pacific
- Atlantic
- Indian
- Arctic
- Southern

c Rivers:
- Nile (Africa)
- Amazon (South America)
- Chang-Jiang (Yangtze) (China)
- Mississippi/Missouri (North America)
- Ob/Irtysh (Asia)

d Continents:
- Asia
- Africa
- North America
- South America
- Antarctica
- Europe
- Oceania

4 Using Atlas Map A, on pages 10–11,

a Give the name and height above sea level of the highest mountain in
- Africa
- South America
- The Alps
- North America

b What sea separates
- Europe from Africa
- Australia from New Zealand
- Africa from Arabia
- China from Japan
- Arabia from India
- South America from the Caribbean
- Vietnam from the Philippines

5 Use Atlas Map A to discover in which continent each of the following rivers are found:

a Tocantins   f Ganges
b Darling   g Niger
c Amur   h Colorado
d Yenisey   i Zambesi
e Danube   j Orinoco

6 Study Table 1.4 which gives the sizes of the seven continents.

a Make a copy of Table 1.4 and calculate the TOTAL area of the seven continents.

b Use your calculator to convert the percentage figures into degrees by multiplying each by 3.6. The calculation for Asia has been done for you.

c Use your degree values to draw a pie chart to show the relative amounts of land belonging to each continent. Use colours and a key to identify each continent.

7 Figure 1.5 lists the teams that took part in the 1998 World Cup.

a Use Atlas Map B (pages 12–13) to help you to locate the countries on a blank country outline of the world. Label the countries on your map using a key if you wish.

b Construct a table to show which continents the different teams represented. To do this draw a table with seven columns, one for each continent. Then use Atlas Map A (pages 10–11) to discover which continent each country belongs to and write it in the correct column.

8 Use Atlas Map B (pages 12–13) to help you locate the following major cities on a blank outline of the world. Label the cities on your map or use a key if you wish.

- New York
- Los Angeles
- Mexico City
- Berlin
- Buenos Aires
- London
- Paris
- Moscow
- Cairo
- Cape Town
- Mumbai (Bombay)
- New Delhi
- Dhaka
- Beijing
- Shanghai
- Tokyo
- Seoul
- Sydney

1.5 The World Cup Contestants in 1998

The Human World

Now look at Atlas Map B on pages 12–13. It shows the countries of the world and the major cities.

In recent years there have been a number of changes to the countries of the world. The USSR, Yugoslavia and Czechoslovakia have all split up into smaller states and West Germany and East Germany have combined to form a single country. Can you think of any other changes that have occurred?

ARCTIC OCEAN
Ellesmere Island
Greenland
Spitsbergen
Norwegian Sea
Arctic Circle
Victoria Island
Great Bear Lake
Baffin Bay
Baffin Island
Iceland
Scand
Yukon
Mt McKinley 6194
Great Slave Lake
Hudson Bay
Labrador
Cape Farewell
British Isles
North Sea
E
Aleutian Is
Gulf of Alaska
Coast Mts
Canadian Shield
Newfoundland
4808 Alps
Vancouver Island
Rocky Mts
Missouri
Lake Superior
Lake Huron
St Lawrence
Mont Blanc
Ap
NORTH
Great Plains
Lake Michigan
Ohio
Tagus
Medit
Mt Whitney 4418
Colorado
AMERICA
Appalachian Mts
Mississippi
North American Basin
Atlas Mts
Tropic of Cancer
Sierra Madre
Rio Grande
Gulf of Mexico
Bahamas
Canary Islands
SAHAR
Cuba
Hoggar
Yucatan
Greater Antilles
Hispaniola
ATLANTIC
AF
Caribbean Sea
Cape Verde Islands
Niger
Ber
Panama Canal
OCEAN
PACIFIC
Orinoco
Guiana Highlands
Gulf of Guinea
Equator
Galapagos Islands
Amazon
OCEAN
Chimborazo 6310
SOUTH
Madeira
Tocantins
Brazil Basin
Marquesas Islands
AMERICA
Brazilian
Angola Basin
St Helena
Tuamotu Islands
Andes
Peru-Chile Trench
Gran Chaco
Paraguay
Paraná
Highlands
Tropic of Capricorn
Ojos del Salado 6908
Aconcagua 6960
Pampas
Argentine Basin
Tristan da Cunha
Goo
Patagonia
Falkland Islands
South Georgia
Tierra del Fuego
C. Horn
Drake Passage
Antarctic Circle
Southeast Pacific Basin
Antarctic Peninsula
Weddell Sea
ANT

KEY

Relief

metres

5000	
3000	
2000	
1000	
500	
200	
0	sea level
200	under sea level
4000	
6000	

Permanent ice

SCALE 1 : 80 000 000

0   800   1600   2400   3200 km

ATLAS MAP A
The world: physical features

© Bartholomew Ltd 1999

A GLOBAL SENSE OF PLACE

RUSSIAN FED.   Arctic Circle   U.S.A.

GREENLAND

ARCTIC

Nuuk (Godthåb)   Reykjavik   ICELAND

NORWAY   SWE.   Oslo   Stockh.   Copenhagen   DEN.

CANADA

Edmonton

Vancouver

Seattle

Winnipeg

UNITED KINGDOM   Dublin   NETH. Amsterdam   GER.   Bonn   BEL. Brussels   LUX.

REP. OF IRELAND   London   SW. AU.   Bern Vienna   Ljubljana

FRANCE   Paris   Sar.   ITALY   Rome

Ottawa   Montreal
Toronto
Chicago   Detroit   Boston
Pittsburgh   New York
Philadelphia

UNITED STATES OF AMERICA

San Francisco

Washington

PORTUGAL   Madrid   SPAIN   Algiers   Tunis

Los Angeles

Lisbon

TUR.

Rabat

MOROCCO

Dallas

Houston

Laayoune

WESTERN SAHARA

Tropic of Cancer

Monterrey

Miami   THE BAHAMAS

MEXICO

MAURITANIA

NIGER

Guadalajara

Havana

Nouakchott

Mexico City

CUBA   Nassau

SENEGAL   Dakar   Bamako   MALI   Niamey

Belmopan   BELIZE

Kingston   HAITI   DOMINICAN REP.   San Juan

THE GAMBIA   Bissau   BUR.   NIGERIA

GUATEMALA   HONDURAS

JAMAICA   PUERTO RICO (USA)

GUINEA-BISSAU   GUINEA   Abuja

Guatemala City   Tegucigalpa

Ouagadougou

EL SALVADOR   NICARAGUA

Conakry   C.D'I.   GH.

Managua

TRINIDAD & TOBAGO

SIERRA LEONE   Yamoussoukro   Lagos

COSTA RICA   Panama City   Caracas   Port of Spain

Freetown   Porto Novo

San José   PANAMA

Monrovia   Accra   Lomé   CAM.

VENEZUELA

LIBERIA   Malabo   Yaoundé

Georgetown   Paramaribo

EQ. G.

GUY.   Cayenne

Libreville   GABON

Bogotá   SUR.   FR.G.

COLOMBIA

Quito

PACIFIC

Galapagos Is (Ec)   ECUADOR

Equator

ATLANTIC

OCEAN

BRAZIL   Recife

PERU

Luanda

Marquesas Is (Fr)

Lima

OCEAN

French Polynesia

La Paz   Brasília

BOLIVIA

Tuamoto Is

Sucre   Belo Horizonte

Europe			Africa	
A.	Andorra		B.	Burundi
ALB.	Albania		BE.	Benin
AUS.	Austria		BUR.	Burkina
BEL.	Belgium		CAM.	Cameroon
BELA.	Belarus		C.D'I.	Côte d'Ivoire
B.H.	Bosnia-Herzegovina		EQ. G.	Equatorial Guinea
CR.	Croatia		GH.	Ghana
CYP.	Cyprus		R.	Rwanda
CZ.	Czech Republic		T.	Togo
DEN.	Denmark			
EST.	Estonia		Asia	
GER.	Germany		AR.	Armenia
H.	Hungary		AZ.	Azerbaijan
LAT.	Latvia		GEO.	Georgia
LITH.	Lithuania		IS.	Israel
LUX.	Luxembourg		JOR.	Jordan
M.	Macedonia		LEB.	Lebanon
MO.	Moldova		U.A.E.	United Arab Emirates
NETH.	Netherlands			
R.F.	Russian Federation		South America	
S.	Slovenia		GUY.	Guyana
SL.	Slovakia		FR.G.	French Guiana
SW.	Switzerland		SUR.	Suriname
YU.	Yugoslavia			

Tropic of Capricorn

PARAGUAY   Rio de Janeiro

Asunción   São Paulo

CHILE

Santiago   ARGENTINA   URUGUAY

Buenos Aires   Montevideo

Cape

Falkland Islands (UK)

N.   Wind

South Georgia (UK)

Antarctic Circle

SCALE 1 : 80 000 000

0   800   1600   2400   3200 km

60° 80° 100° 120° 140° 160° 80°

Arctic Circle

AN

RUSSIAN FEDERATION

60°

St Petersburg
in

Nizhniy
Novgorod
Moscow

Yekaterinburg

Omsk

Novosibirsk

Minsk
A

Samara

Akmola

Kiev

URAINE

Chisinau
ANA
ucharest
de

GARIA

KAZAKSTAN

MONGOLIA

Ulan Bator

Harbin

Shenyang

40°

Tiflis
GEO.
AR
Ankara
Yerevan

AZ

Bishkek

KYRGYZSTAN

Almaty

Beijing

Dalian N. KOREA
Pyongyang
Tianjin Seoul
S. KOREA

Tokyo
Osaka

TURKEY

Baku

UZBEKISTAN

Tashkent
TURKMEN-
ISTAN

TAJIKISTAN
Dushanbe

Lanzhou

Xi'an

JAPAN

CYP.

SYRIA
LEB.

Damascus

Ashgabat

Tehran

Kabul

Islamabad

PACIFIC

Jerusalem
IS JOR.
Amman

IRAQ

Baghdad

IRAN

AFGHAN-
ISTAN

Lahore

New
Delhi

CHINA

Nanjing
Wuhan
Chengdu

Shanghai

Chongqing

OCEAN

Cairo

KUWAIT

Kuwait

NEPAL

BHUTAN

40°

Delhi
Kathmandu

Taibei

Tropic of Cancer

EGYPT

SAUDI

Riyadh

BAHRAIN
QATAR

U.A.E.

Karachi

Muscat

Dhaka
BANGLA-
DESH

Guangzhou

20°

TAIWAN

ARABIA

OMAN

Calcutta

Hong
Kong

INDIA

MYANMAR

LAOS

Hanoi

ERITREA

YEMEN

Sana

Mumbai
(Bombay)

Vientiane

VIETNAM

Manila

PHILIPPINES

Khartoum

Asmara

Yangon

Northern
Marianas
(USA)

MARSHALL
ISLANDS

SUDAN

Addis
Ababa

DJIBOUTI

Chennai
(Madras)

THAILAND

Bangkok

CAMBODIA

Ho Chi Minh

ETHIOPIA

SOMALIA

Phnom
Penh

PALAU

UGANDA

Kampala

Colombo

SRI
LANKA

BRUNEI

Kuala Lumpur **MALAYSIA**

FED. STATES OF
MICRONESIA

RATIC
NGOR

Kigali

Nairobi

MALDIVES

SINGAPORE

Equator

0°

B.

Bujumbura

KENYA

Mogadishu

SEYCHELLES

NAURU

KIRIBATI

TANZANIA

Dodoma

Dar es Salaam

INDIAN

INDONESIA

PAPUA
NEW
GUINEA

SOLOMON
ISLANDS

TUVALU

Lilongwe

COMOROS

OCEAN

Jakarta

AMBIA

MOZAMBIQUE

saka

Port
Moresby

Harare

Antananarivo

VANUATU

FIJI

ZIMBABWE

MADAGASCAR

MAURITIUS

New
Caledonia
(Fr.)

Suva

20°

NA

ria
urg

Maputo

Mbabane
SWAZILAND

Nouméa

Tropic of Capricorn

F
HA

LESOTHO

Maseru

AUSTRALIA

Brisbane

Perth

Sydney

Adelaide

Canberra

Auckland

NEW
ZEALAND

40°

Melbourne

Wellington

Kerguelen
(Fr)

60°

Antarctic Circle

ANTARCTICA

60° 80° 100° 120° 140° 160° 80°

2 Finding your way around the world

Latitude and longitude

When studying geography at a global scale, we use atlas maps such as Atlas Maps A and B a great deal. To help us locate places, an imaginary grid is drawn over the Earth's surface (see Skills Box 1).

These lines run around the world parallel to the Equator and are called lines of **latitude**. There are also imaginary lines running between the north and south poles called lines of **longitude**. Just like northings and eastings on an Ordnance Survey map, the lines of latitude and longitude help us to locate places with accuracy. Study Skills Box 1 to discover how to use latitude and longitude to find the location of places.

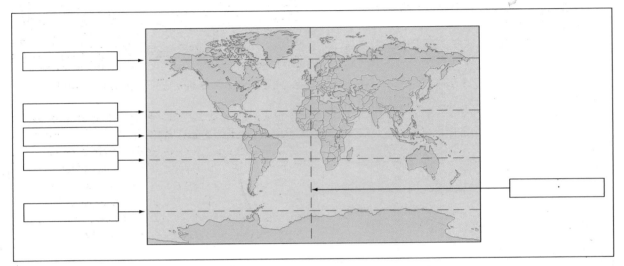

2.1 Imaginary lines of latitude and longitude help us to locate where places are in the world

1 Study Figure 2.1. It shows a number of important lines of latitude and longitude. Draw these lines onto a blank map of the world and use Atlas Map A (pages 10–11) to help you label them.

2 Study the information in Skills Box 1.

a What is special about the Equator?

b How can the Equator be used to split the world into two halves?

c What name is given to the 0° line of longitude?

d How can the 0° line of longitude be used to split the world into two halves?

e The text in Skills Box 1 describes how to use latitude and longitude to locate Halkirk. Describe in a similar way how to use latitude and longitude to locate the town of Wick in Scotland. Include a simple sketch map as part of your description.

3 Find out about the importance of the Tropics of Cancer and Capricorn and the Arctic and Antarctic Circles. Look them up in dictionaries or encyclopedias (books or CD-ROMs).

4 Use Atlas Map A (pages 10–11) to discover which mountains are located at the following references. For example, 37N 118W is Mt Whitney, USA.
- 36N 77E
- 01S 79W
- 03S 37E
- 00 37E
- 46N 7E

5 Use Atlas Map B (pages 12–13) to discover which cities are located at the following references. For example, 41N 74W is New York, USA.
- 36N 51E
- 56N 38E
- 6S 36E
- 19N 99W
- 35S 149E
- 45N 76W
- 16S 48W
- 40N 116E
- 14N 101E
- 34S 18E

SKILLS BOX 1

Finding places using latitude and longitude

When lines of latitude and longitude are drawn on a map they form a grid pattern, very much like a pattern of squares.

By stating the latitude and then the longitude of a place, it becomes much easier to find. On the map (below) Point A is very easy to find because it is exactly latitude 58° North of the Equator and longitude 4° West of the Greenwich Meridian (58°N 4°W).

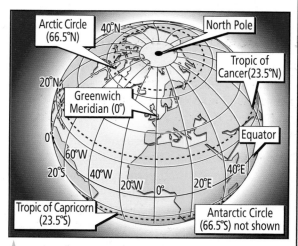

Lines of latitude and longitude on the globe

To be even more accurate in locating a place, each degree of latitude and longitude can also be divided into smaller units called **minutes** ('). There are 60 minutes in each degree. On the map opposite Halkirk is one half (or 30/60ths) of the way past latitude 58N, and halfway of the way past 3°W. Its latitude is therefore, 58 degrees 30 minutes North and its longitude is 30 degrees 30 minutes West. This can be shortened to 58°30'N, 30°30'W.

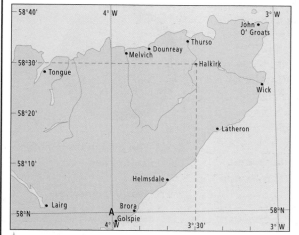

Locating Point A and Halkirk in Scotland

How the world is divided by the Equator and the Greenwich Meridian

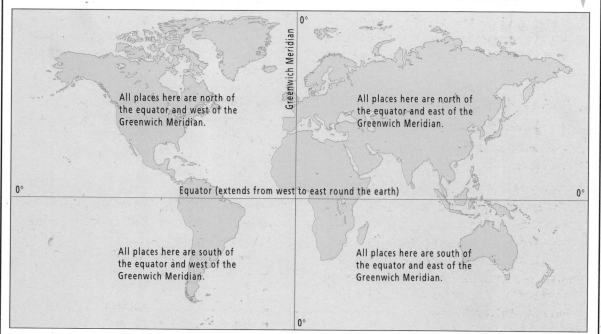

All places here are north of the equator and west of the Greenwich Meridian.

All places here are north of the equator and east of the Greenwich Meridian.

Equator (extends from west to east round the earth)

All places here are south of the equator and west of the Greenwich Meridian.

All places here are south of the equator and east of the Greenwich Meridian.

What's the time around the world?

The Earth orbits the sun and, as it does so, it rotates on its axis. As the Earth rotates, one half of it is lit (daytime) whereas the other half is in darkness (night). If clocks were set at the same time across the world, the working day, from 9am–5pm, would be daylight in some places but during darkness in others. For this reason countries developed their own local time.

With the beginnings of international travel, there was a need to organise all the different local times around the world. Look at Figure 2.3. Notice that the world is divided into a number of time zones. This means that, in theory, at any point on the Earth's surface, when the sun is highest in the sky, it is 12 noon. Notice that the time zones are broadly parallel to the lines of longitude. This is because the Earth rotates on its axis from west to east.

If you have flown you will be used to the idea of adjusting your watch to 'local time'. You will also have experienced 'jet lag' as your body tries to adjust. If you wanted to travel west from the the UK, you would need to adjust your watch accordingly. For example, if you left London at noon, the local time in Washington, USA would be 7am because Washington is 5 hours 'behind' London (see Figure 2.2). Travelling from London, in the opposite direction, towards the Russian Federation and Asia, you would have to adjust your watch forward. Study Figure 2.2 to discover that, for example, noon in London is 3pm (+3 hours) in Moscow.

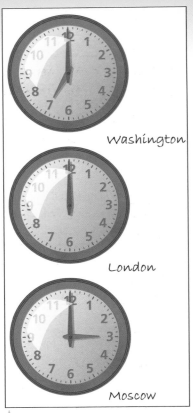

Washington

London

Moscow

▲ **2.2 The time in Washington, London, Moscow**

▼ **2.3 World time zones**

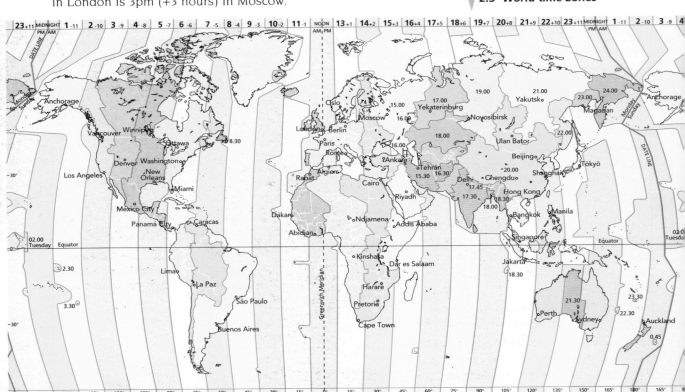

6 Look at Table 2.4. It gives a number of British Airways departure times from London (Heathrow).

a Make a copy of Table 2.4 and use Figure 2.3 to complete the column giving the length (flight time) of each departure.

▼ **2.4 British Airways departures from London (Heathrow)**

Flight no.	Departure	Destination	Arrival (local time)	Flight time
BA2249	10.15	Caracas	14.35	8hrs 20mins
BA11	12.00	Perth	14.10 (next day)	
BA293	12.35	Miami	17.00	
BA764	13.35	Oslo	16.40	
BA135	13.50	Riyadh	22.10	
BA31	15.25	Manila	14.10 (next day)	
BA007	16.30	Tokyo	12.15 (next day)	
BA7991	21.05	Vancouver	22.35	
BA59	21.15	Cape Town	09.45 (next day)	
BA145	21.55	New Dehli	11.10 (next day)	

(Source: British Airways)

b On a blank map of the world, locate all the city destinations. Use Atlas Map B on pages 12–13 to help you.

3 Rich world, poor world: an introduction to development

You have discovered that the world is a place of great physical contrasts. There are magnificent mountains, hot, dusty deserts and vast oceans. It is also a place of great human contrasts (see Photos 3.1 and 3.2).

Some people are lucky to have a comfortable standard of living, with a home, a job and plenty to eat and drink. Others (the bulk of the world's population) are much less fortunate. Nearly a quarter of the world's population live in **absolute poverty**. This means that they cannot afford enough food, shelter or medicine.

In geography, we use two very important terms when we talk about the rich world and the poor world. The MEDC (more economically developed countries) includes the countries of Europe, North America, Japan, Australia and New Zealand, and some countries in Asia, Africa and South America (Figure 3.3). The LEDC (less economically developed countries) includes most of Africa and Asia and some countries in South America (Figure 3.3).

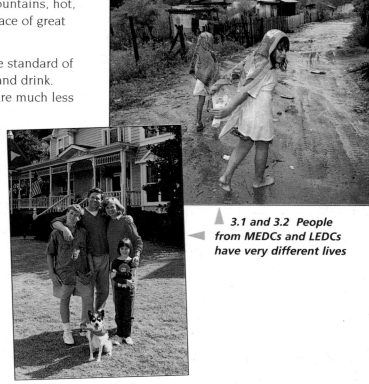

▲ **3.1 and 3.2 People from MEDCs and LEDCs have very different lives**

1 Study Photos 3.1 and 3.2. For each photo describe the scene in as much detail as you can. What are the signs of wealth and poverty?

2 Study Figure 3.3. Draw up a table with two columns, one for 'Rich World' and one for 'Poor World'. Use Atlas Map B (pages 12–13) to help you choose 25 countries to put in each column.

3 What is meant by the term 'absolute poverty'?

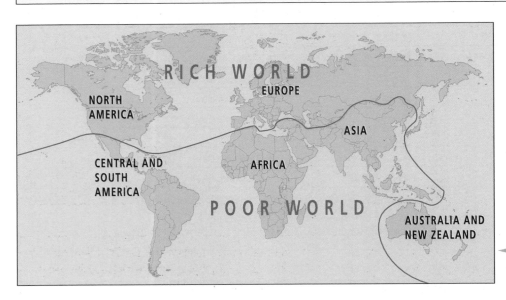

◀ *3.3 The Brandt Line divides the world into rich and poor*

What is development?

The word 'development' is hard to define. It is all about improvements in people's quality of life. This may involve giving aid to people in the form of food and technology, or simply enabling them to help themselves. Some of these issues will be studied later in this book in Chapter 3.

How can development be measured?

The most common measure of development is wealth. Wealth is usually measured by a country's **gross national product (GNP)**. This is the value of all goods and services produced in a country. It is usually expressed in 'US dollars per capita'. This means that the total value of goods and services (converted to US dollars) has been divided by the total number of people living in that country.

Look at Figure 3.4. Notice that there are great contrasts in wealth across the world. Are the richest and poorest countries the same as you thought?

SKILLS BOX 2
Drawing a choropleth map

A choropleth map is a map that uses different colours to show information. It is useful in showing patterns. A good choropleth map should make the pattern immediately obvious.

Look at Figure 3.4 to see some of the features of a choropleth map:

- the data is arranged into a number of groups (4–8 groups is the ideal number)

- each group has a colour or shade, increasing in darkness as the value increases. Figure 3.4 uses shades of green. One possible sequence of `colours is yellow-orange-red-brown-black.

- there is no overlap in values from one group to the next

- areas without data are usually left blank (on Figure 3.4 a light purple tint is used)

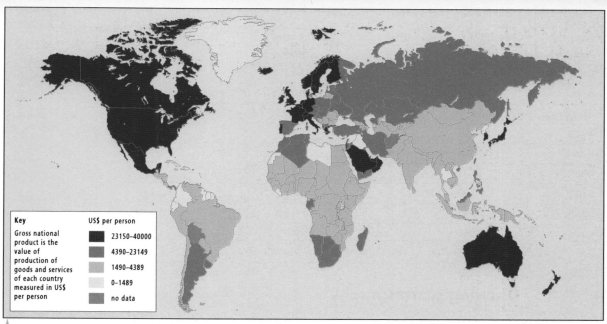

Key

Gross national product is the value of production of goods and services of each country measured in US$ per person

US$ per person

23150–40000

4390–23149

1490–4389

0–1489

no data

▲ *3.4 World GNP (US dollars per capita)*

4 Figure 3.4 is a type of map called a choropleth map. You came across these maps in Book 2. Look at Skills Box 2 to discover how a choropleth map is drawn.

a Draw a choropleth map to show adult literacy (the ability to read and write) for those countries listed in Table 3.6 (page 20). Notice in Table 3.6 that the adult literacy rate is expressed as a percentage.

Colour each country on a blank map of the world using the following colour key:

Adult literacy rate

95.1% and over	black
80.1–95%	brown
65.1–80%	red
50.1–65%	orange
under 50%	yellow

Give your map a title and include a key.

b Compare your map to that of GNP (Figure 3.4).

Do the rich countries appear to have the highest or lowest levels of literacy? Why do you think that is so? Can you see any exceptions to the general rule?

5 Let's look further at the relationship between GNP and adult literacy.

a Make a copy of Table 3.6. There are two columns with the titles GNP rank and adult literacy rank.

b In these two new columns rank the GNP values and the adult literacy values, with the highest value being ranked 1 and the lowest 10.

c Plot the rankings on a copy of the graph (Figure 3.5). This is a scattergraph. Use the graphs in Skills Box 3 to plot a best fit line. Using the information in Skills Box 3, attempt to answer the following questions:

d Is there a good relationship between GNP and adult literacy?

e There are two residuals. Which countries are they?

f Try to suggest why the two countries are far away from the best fit line.

▼ *3.5 Graph axes for Activity 5*

3.6 Is there a relationship between GNP and adult literacy?

Country	GNP ($per capita)	GNP rank	Adult literacy (%)	Adult literacy rank
Algeria	1600		57.4	
Bangladesh	240		36.4	
Brazil	3640		81.9	
China	620		79.3	
India	340		49.9	
Iran	1033		64.9	
Mexico	3320		88.6	
Nigeria	260		52.5	
Saudi Arabia	7040		60.6	
USA	26980		99	

SKILLS BOX 3

Drawing scattergraphs

We draw a scattergraph to discover if there is a relationship between two sets of data.

Scattergraphs plot the two sets of data to create a scatter of points on a graph. A value on one axis meets with a value on the other axis to form each point or cross on the graph (see graph a).

If the points form a pattern, a best-fit line can be drawn bisecting the points. The relationship can then be described (see graph b and graph c).

Graph a ▶

▼ Graph b

Graph c ◀

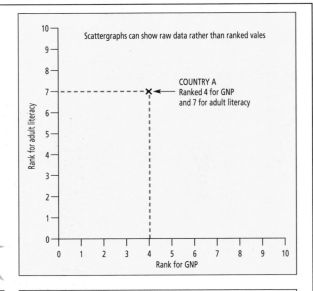

Scattergraphs can show raw data rather than ranked vales

COUNTRY A
Ranked 4 for GNP and 7 for adult literacy

Rank for adult literacy / Rank for GNP

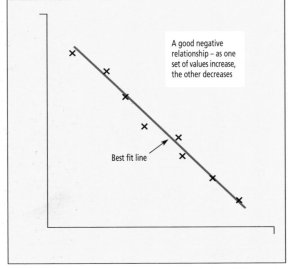

A residual point away from the main trend (Best fit line)

A good positive relationship – as one set of values increase, so does the other

Best fit line

A good negative relationship – as one set of values increase, the other decreases

Best fit line

Weather and climate

Weather and climate vary a great deal around the world. Some places experience extremes of hot and cold and wet and dry, and people have to adapt to live in these conditions. Climates change over long periods of time and recently people have become concerned about human activity leading to global warming.

1 Extreme weather

In October 1987 parts of southern England were hit by an unusually powerful storm that some people called a hurricane. High winds tore roofs off houses and flattened 15 million trees (see Photo 1.1). Thirty people lost their lives and an estimated £2 billion worth of damage was caused. During the storm, the wind gusted to over 120 km per hour.

In early 1990, northern Europe was again hit by powerful storms. Some 230 people were killed– mostly by trees falling on to cars. These storms caused more damage than any other natural disaster in history. They are good examples of extreme weather.

Occasionally we hear that weather records have been broken. You learned in Book 1 that August 1995 was the hottest and sunniest August ever recorded in the UK. Records are broken and new ones established all around the world.

▲ *1.1 The 1987 storm caused chaos in London and the rest of southern England*

▼ *1.2 Global weather extremes*

1 Highest wind gust	372 km per hour	Mt Washington, USA (1934)
2 Hottest place	57.8°C	Al' Aziziyah, Libya (1922)
3 Largest hailstone	1.02 kg	Gopalganj, Bangladesh (1986)
4 Highest annual rainfall	26,462 mm	Cherrapunji, India (1860–1)
5 Coldest place	-89.2°C	Vostok, Antarctica (1983)
6 Highest annual snowfall	31, 102 mm	Mt Rainier, USA (1971–2)
7 Highest daily rainfall	1,870 mm	La Reunion, near Madagascar (1952)
8 Driest place	400 years of drought	Atacama Desert, South America
9 Sunniest place	4,300 hrs a year	Sahara Desert, Africa
10 Most rapid temperature change	-20°C to +7°C in two minutes	S. Dakota, USA (1943)

(Source: Collins, 1996 Weather William Burroughs, et al.)

1 Study Photo 1.1.

a Describe the scene in the photo.

b What other damage do you think strong winds could cause in towns and in the countryside?

2 Study the information in Table 1.2 and locate the places using Atlas Maps A and B (pages 10–11 and 12–13).

2 World climates

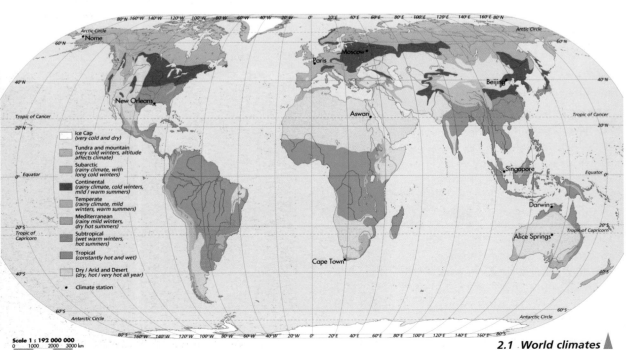

2.1 World climates ▲

Scale 1 : 192 000 000
0   1000   2000   3000 km

© Bartholomew Ltd 1999

2.2 The effect of the angle of the sun's energy on the surface temperatures

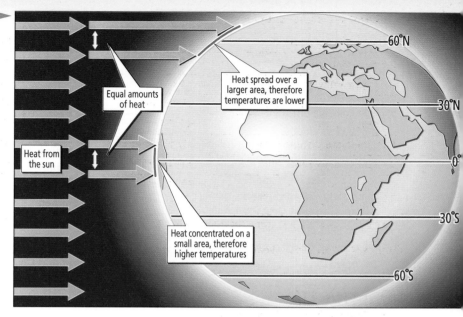

The word climate means the average weather of a place, usually taken over a period of 30 years. Look at Figure 2.1. Notice that there are many different climates around the world. Locate the UK and find the colour in the key. It tells us that the UK has a **temperate climate**. This means that the climate is between tropical and tundra – it is not one of extremes. Those places with a temperate climate tend to have fairly mild winters and warm, but not hot, summers. Look back to the map and notice that much of western Europe has the same type of climate.

Some countries have several different climates. Locate Australia on Figure 2.1. Notice that most of Australia has a 'hot, arid and desert' climate. However around the coast there are four other climate types. A similar variety of climates can be seen in the USA, Brazil and even in smaller countries such as Italy.

Why is there a variety of world climates?

There are several reasons for the variety of climates on Figure 2.1.

- The hottest climates are within the Tropics. Here the sun is almost directly overhead for much of the year and it is much more powerful than in higher latitudes (see Figure 2.2).

- The intense heat around the Equator causes the air to rise. The air here is very moist and it rises to form tall clouds which produce large amounts of rain.

- At about 30 degrees north and south, there is a zone of deserts. This area experiences clear skies and very little cloud. The air is dry and so rain is rare.

- Outside the Tropics and with increasing latitude, the climate gradually becomes cooler. Temperate becomes Subarctic which in turn becomes Arctic. This change is mainly because the sun becomes less powerful (Figure 2.2) as distance increases from the Equator.

- Continental climates are found in the centre of large land masses. Away from the influence of the sea, there is only a low amount of rainfall. Summers are hot and and winters are often very cold.

2.3 A cold, frosty day in Norway

1 Look at Table 2.4.

a Make a careful copy of Table 2.4.

b Use the key in Figure 2.1 to complete the first two columns.

c Now complete the third column giving an example of an area or country that experiences each type of climate. Use Atlas Maps A and B (pages 10–11 and 12–13) to help you. Do not choose a country more than once and try to find parts of the world that are different from those likely to be chosen by your classmates.

2 Study Figure 2.1.

a Make a copy of the different climates of Australia on to a blank outline of the country. Use colours of your choice. Remember to explain each colour in a key. Use Atlas Map B (pages 12–13) to locate and label Australia's main cities.

b What is the most widespread climate in Australia?

c Why do you think so much of Australia has a desert climate?

2.4 Summary of world climates

Climate type	Characteristics	World location
Ice cap		
Tundra		
	Rainy with long, cold winters	
Continental		
	Rainy with mild winters and warm summers	
	Rainy with mild winters and dry, hot summers	
Sub-tropical		
	Constantly hot and wet	
	Dry/arid and Desert	

2.5 Climate data for Darwin and Alice Springs, Australia

Darwin	J	F	M	A	M	J	J	A	S	O	N	D
Max. Temp. (°C)	32	32	33	33	33	31	31	32	33	34	34	33
Min. Temp. (°C)	25	25	25	24	23	21	19	21	23	25	26	26
Rainfall (mm)	386	312	254	97	15	3	0	3	13	51	119	239

Alice Springs	J	F	M	A	M	J	J	A	S	O	N	D
Max. Temp. (°C)	36	35	32	27	23	19	19	23	27	31	34	36
Min. Temp. (°C)	21	21	17	12	8	5	4	6	9	14	18	20
Rainfall (mm)	43	33	28	10	15	13	8	8	8	18	31	38

(Source   E.A. Pearce The World Weather Guide   Hutchinson)

3 Hurricanes

How are hurricanes formed?

Hurricanes are huge storms often over 250 km wide and moving at speeds of about 80 km per hour. They are one of the most powerful natural hazards on Earth.

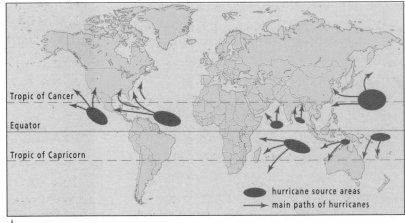

3.1 Hurricane source areas and paths

A hurricane releases energy equal to the explosion of a hydrogen bomb every minute of its life. The ideal location for a hurricane to form is over the ocean somewhere near the Equator. As the warm, moist air begins to rise huge thunderclouds are formed (Figure 3.2). The rotation of the Earth then causes the whole storm to rotate, in a spiral.

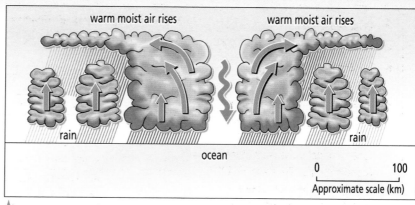

▲ **3.2 A cross-section through a hurricane**

---

1 Study Figure 3.1.

a On a blank world outline draw carefully the eight hurricane source areas and the arrows indicating the common tracks (paths) of hurricanes.

b The eight areas are listed below. Use Atlas Map A (pages 10–11) to label each one correctly on your map using a key if you wish.
   1   central Indian Ocean
   2   western Atlantic Ocean
   3   Arabian Sea
   4   western Pacific Ocean (off Japan)
   5   Bay of Bengal
   6   Banda Sea (off northern Australia)
   7   eastern Pacific (off Central America)
   8   south Pacific (off Solomon Islands)

c Use Atlas Map B (pages 12–13) to help you locate and label some of the countries affected by hurricanes.

2 Figure 3.2 shows a simplified cross-section through a hurricane. Make a copy of Figure 3.2 adding the following labels in their correct places.
   ● heavy rainfall
   ● central 'eye' of the hurricane formed by sinking air
   ● rapidly rising air, forming tall clouds
   ● outer area with smaller clouds and lighter rain

What is the hurricane hazard?

Hurricanes can cause tremendous damage and destruction when they cross islands or hit coastal areas. There are three main hazards associated with hurricanes.

● Strong winds. These will destroy homes, uproot trees and flatten crops (see Photo 3.3). Power and telephone lines will often be brought down, causing additional hardship.

● Heavy rainfall. Torrential rain may bring up to 300 mm of rain in a single day. (This is equivalent to half the average annual rainfall for London.) Rivers may be unable to cope

▲ **3.3 Damage to house in Puerto Rico due to strong winds**

with the extra water, and flooding may occur.

● Storm surge. An intense storm can whip-up the sea and lead to a rise in sea level called a **storm surge**. A surge can cause sea level to rise over 10 metres above its normal height, causing serious flooding to low-lying coastal areas.

3.4 Survivors struggle along the Pan-American highway near Chinandegan in Nicaragua ▶

Case Study: Hurricane Mitch

In November 1998 the Central American countries of Honduras and Nicaragua were hit by one of the most powerful storms of the century. The intense storm, called Hurricane Mitch, brought torrential rain for three days, and the floods and mudslides resulted in a death toll of over 11,000 people.

Communications were in ruins as most main roads and bridges had been washed away by floodwater. The survivors faced several days without food, water and shelter. Diseases such as cholera soon broke out, causing yet more deaths.

Both Honduras and Nicaragua are very poor countries and this fact contributed to the scale of the disaster. A lack of helicopters, poor communications and few emergency provisions meant that the relief operation was painfully slow.

The effect of the disaster will be felt for several years to come. Many farmers lost their livelihoods because most of the countries' banana plantations were swept away. It will take a very long time to rebuild the thousands of houses, roads and bridges that were destroyed.

In common with many LEDCs, Honduras and Nicaragua have huge debts, so they have little money available for rebuilding. Fortunately, immediately after the disaster many countries and charities launched campaigns to raise money for the victims of the hurricane.

3.5 Extracts from newspapers on Hurricane Mitch ▼

'Honduras has suffered enormous damage from flood and landslides, from the eastern coastal marshes to deep within its wild interior. The scale of the problem is huge. At least 600,000 people have fled their homes. Many others have no food or water, and the roads and bridges that would normally supply aid simply no longer exist.' 'Everywhere there are the dead, waiting to be buried or burned (to reduce the threat of cholera), the twisted corpses protruding obscenely from the mud covered-legacy that Mitch has left.

Telegraph (5/11/98)

'Honduras is worst affected. Nearly the whole country – 85% – is under water, and 75% of agriculture has been destroyed. The capital, Tegucigalpa, is ruined, with virtually no communications with the outside world. Thousands of houses and 73 bridges have been destroyed.'

Independent (6/11/98)

Forecasting hurricanes

Satellites, aeroplanes and radar can be used to track hurricanes as they move across the world, and their courses can be plotted. As a hurricane approaches a country, warnings are issued. People may be encouraged to cover windows with shutters, take pets inside, stock-up on food and water and, if necessary, evacuate the area.

3 In this activity you will plot the course of Hurricane Mitch. You will need to use a copy or tracing of Figure 3.6 and the data in Table 3.7. Work in pencil first before using colours and ink.

a Plot carefully the course of the hurricane using the positions given in Table 3.7. Notice that the first part of the course has been done for you.

▼ **3.7 Hurricane Mitch – plotting data**

Date	Time	Latitude	Longitude
22 Oct	1500	12.00N	78.00W
23 Oct	0300	12.00N	77.10W
24 Oct	1500	13.90N	77.00W
25 Oct	0300	15.10N	78.20W
25 Oct	1800	16.40N	80.30W
26 Oct	0300	16.40N	81.50W
26 Oct	1500	16.70N	82.90W
28 Oct	0300	16.50N	85.60W
29 Oct	0300	16.30N	86.00W
30 Oct	1500	15.30N	86.20W
31 Oct	0300	14.40N	87.30W
31 Oct	1500	14.50N	88.70W
01 Nov	1500	14.90N	91.60W
03 Nov	2100	19.40N	91.30W
04 Nov	1500	21.80N	88.30W
05 Nov	0000	23.80N	85.40W

(Source: Purdue University, USA. Downloaded from the Internet)

b When you have finished, use a colour to show the course of the hurricane more clearly.

c When did the hurricane hit Honduras?

d Through which other countries did the hurricane pass?

e Write a few sentences describing the course of Hurricane Mitch.

f Do you think it was easy to predict the course of the hurricane? Explain your answer.

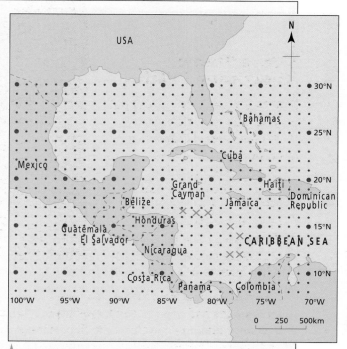

▲ **3.6 Hurricane tracking chart**

4 Read the Case Study on Hurricane Mitch.

a Make a list of some of the immediate effects of Hurricane Mitch on Honduras and Nicaragua.

b Electricity was cut off from many homes. Imagine that electricity was cut off from your home for a few days. What effect would it have on your family?

c What effect did the hurricane have on communications? How did this cause problems in the days and weeks that followed?

d Describe the effects that the hurricane had on farming.

e Suggest some of the longer-term effects of the hurricane on the people of Honduras and Nicaragua.

f If you were in charge of a large sum of money raised to help victims of the disaster, what would you spend the money on. Make a list in rank order and then give reasons for your list.

4 Climate change

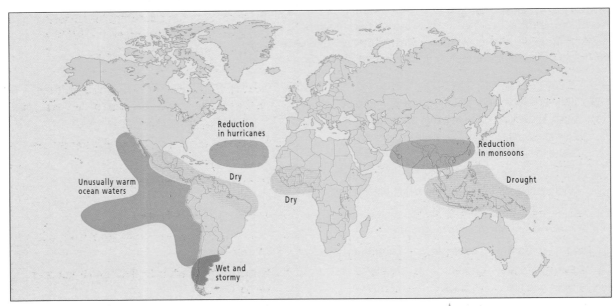

4.1 Some effects of El Nino (June–September 1997)

Climates have changed a great deal in the past. For example, it was only 12,000 years ago that much of northern Europe was covered by ice. In the hot and dry Sahara desert there is evidence that the climate was once much wetter than it is today.

In recent years two aspects of climate change – the El Nino effect and global warming – have become important global issues.

El Nino

El Nino is the name given to a climatic event that alters the normal patterns of weather in the Tropics. During an El Nino event, the normally cold waters off the west coast of South America experience a rise in temperature of between 5 and 10 degrees celsius that lasts for a few months. This has an effect on the major winds in the region which, in turn, causes unusual and severe weather throughout the Tropics (Figure 4.1).

4.2 El Nino can cause severe drought and the failure of harvests

It is called El Nino because its effects are usually first felt off the coast of Peru (Spanish speaking) around Christmas time. El Nino is a Spanish phrase meaning 'the little one'.

Peru depends greatly on its anchovy fishing industry. Anchovies are small fish (you may have eaten them on a pizza) that thrive in the normally cold waters off the Peruvian coast. During an El Nino episode, the warmer waters drastically reduce the numbers of anchovies and Peru's economy is hit very hard.

An El Nino event occurs on average once every 7 years and its effects last for about a year. In 1997/98 many extreme weather events were blamed on its influence (Table 4.3).

Scientists are still not sure why El Nino occurs. However, ocean temperatures can be measured using satellites, making it possible, to some extent, to forecast an El Nino event. The next El Nino is due in 2004 – watch out for it!

4.3 Severe and unusual weather resulting from El Nino 1997/98 ▼

India	Earliest onset of the monsoon rains for 97 years
New Zealand	Warmest summer for 60 years
Canada	Warmest spring on record
Indonesia	Widespread forest fires devastate areas of rainforest
Peru	Torrential rain causing floods and landslides
Australia	Drought affects wheat harvests
Ecuador	Torrential rain floods over 15,000 homes
South Africa	Severe drought damages harvest
Papua New Guinea	Drought leads to famine as harvests fail
California, USA	Torrential rain causes floods and landslides
Malaysia	Widespread forest fires devastate areas of brushwood and forest
Somalia/Ethiopia	Devastating floods

1 For this activity you will need a blank outline map of the world. Study Table 4.3.

a Locate on your world outline map the countries whose severe and unusual weather in 1997/98 was thought to result from El Nino. Use Atlas Map B (pages 12–13) to help you locate the places.

b Make up symbols and use colours to illustrate the weather events. Add labels to describe each event or include the details in a key.

c Draw on to your map the Tropic of Cancer and the Tropic of Capricorn.

d Make up a title for your map.

2 Study the text about El Nino.

a What does 'El Nino' mean in English and why is it so named?

b Where are the effects of El Nino first felt and what happens?

c To what extent did the effects of the 1997/98 El Nino affect weather within the tropics only?

d How is it possible to forecast El Nino?

e What do you think countries likely to be affected by El Nino in 2004 could do to prepare themselves?

▼ **4.4 Forest fires in Indonesia caused by El Nino**

Global warming

One of the most important issues of our time is that of global warming. Over the last hundred years the average temperature of the world has increased by 0.5°C. This increase may not sound very much, but it is enough to change climates, alter patterns of rainfall and lead to the melting of ice caps and glaciers (Photo 4.5).

One of the most important facts about global warming is that, unlike other forms of climate change, it is probably due, at least in part, to the effects of human activity.

What is causing global warming?

The atmosphere (the air above our heads) consists of liquids, gases and solid particles such as dust. When heat is lost from the Earth's surface, the air absorbs some of it, preventing it being lost to space. In this way, the Earth is kept warm enough to support life, just like plants are kept warm in a greenhouse. It is this absorption and storage of heat that is known as the **greenhouse effect** (see Figure 4.6).

3 Read the text about global warming.

a What is global warming?

b How much has the average temperature of the world increased during the last 100 years?

c In what way is the current global warming different from climatic changes that have happened in the past?

4 Make a copy of Figure 4.6 and select labels from the following list to complete the empty boxes:
- Burning fossil fuels in power stations and factories gives off carbon dioxide
- Sun's heat directed towards the Earth
- Some heat from the Earth escapes to space
- Nitrous oxides from vehicle exhausts
- Methane released from animal waste and padi rice farms
- Some heat from the sun is reflected back into space
- Burning forests adds carbon dioxide to the atmosphere
- Heat given off from the Earth is stored within the atmosphere

▲ **4.5** *Ice thawing in the summer at Magnetic Island, Antarctica*

4.6 The greenhouse effect

During the last two hundred years, human activity has led to increased pollution of the skies. Gases which are effective in absorbing heat have been emitted from factory chimneys and power stations (Photo 4.8). These gases, which include carbon dioxide, nitrous oxides and methane, are called **greenhouse gases** because they increase the greenhouse effect. Scientists believe that it is this increased pollution that is responsible for the current trend of global warming.

What are the possible effects of global warming?

Whilst most scientists agree that global warming is happening, there is much disagreement about the likely

5 Study Table 4.7.

4.7 Top ten countries with the highest industrial emissions of carbon dioxide (1992) (million metric tonnes) ▼

USA	4,881,349
China	2,667,982
Russian Federation	2,103,132
Japan	1,093,470
Germany	878,136
India	769,440
Ukraine	611,342
UK	566,246
Canada	409,862
Italy	407,701

(Source: World Resources Institute)

a Draw a bar chart to show the emissions of carbon dioxide for the ten countries.

b Many countries are putting pressure on the USA to reduce its emissions. Do you think this is fair?

c China and India are likely to become much more industrialised in the future. Why do you think scientists are concerned about this?

4.8 Pollution from industry in China

effects that it will have on our lives. The atmosphere is incredibly complicated – not even the most advanced computer in the world can model how it works.

There are a number of possible harmful effects of global warming.

- Rising sea levels. It seems likely that global sea levels will rise as glaciers and ice sheets start to melt. Rises of between 10 cm and 25 cm have already been recorded over the last 100 years.

- Extreme weather. Weather extremes such as floods, hurricanes and heatwaves may be more common.

- Global vegetation belts may shift. As some parts of the world become hotter, so the belts of desert, grasslands and forests may shift poleward. This will affect farming and people's livelihoods.

However, it is not all bad news. In some regions of the world, global warming will actually bring benefits. For example, crops that thrive in warm weather, like grapes, wheat and barley, will be able to be grown more easily in northern Europe, Canada and in parts of the Russian Federation.

Look at Table 4.9 to read about some of the possible effects of global warming around the world.

Can global warming be reduced?

Whilst nothing can be done about the warming that has already taken place, it is possible to reduce levels of pollution and, therefore, reduce global warming in the future.

In 1997 at Kyoto in Japan, 38 countries signed an agreement to reduce emissions. However, those countries that signed the agreement only contributed 25% of total emissions. A number of big polluters such as the USA, India and China have yet to agree to reductions because they fear that their economies would suffer if their industries had to become cleaner.

Until international agreements are reached and implemented, global warming seems likely to continue.

▼ *4.9 The possible impact of global warming on the world*

Country or region	Possible impact of global warming
UK	The south may become hotter and drier, and the north wetter. Storms may be more common.
Maldives	These low-lying islands could disappear
Bangladesh	9% of the country could be permanently submerged
Nile Valley, Egypt	15% could be submerged. This is Egypt's only area of productive farmland.
Sahel, North Africa	Increased risk of soil erosion, drought and famine
USA (Mid-West)	Drier climate could reduce the grain harvest
Southern Canada	Drier, warmer climate could increase the grain harvest
China	Increased rainfall could increase rice yields
Alps	Melting of glaciers could harm the tourist industry
Florida coast, USA	Increased risk of flooding from storm surges

(Sources: various Internet sites, including BBC, CNN, World Resources Institute, FOE, IPCC)

6 Study Table 4.9.

a Use Atlas Maps A and B (pages 10–11 and 12–13) to locate the places listed in Table 4.9 on to a blank world outline.

b Now add labels to describe the possible effects of global warming at each of the locations. You could write your labels in boxes if you wish.

c Use colours and simple sketches or symbols to make your map look attractive.

Population

At the start of the 21st century there are about 6,000,000,000 people living in the world. Every year the population grows by another 90 million. The population of the world is unevenly spread – some parts are more densely populated than others. Some people choose to move from one place to another in search of a job or a better quality of life. However, occasionally some people are forced to move and they become refugees.

1 Population distribution

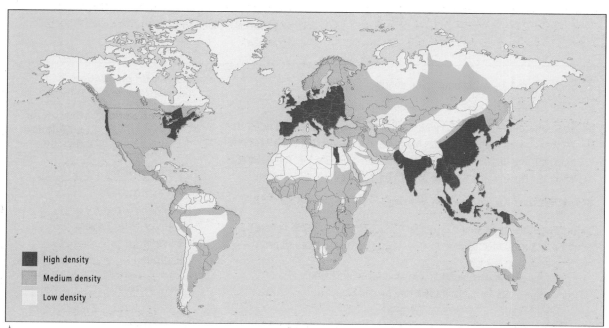

High density
Medium density
Low density

▲ *1.1 World population density and distribution*

Look at Figure 1.1. Notice that it is an example of a choropleth map, with darker colours indicating higher values. Look at the key to see that the colours show population density. Population density is the number of people per square kilometre.

Notice that the population of the world is unevenly spread. There are some areas that have a very high density such as India, eastern China and much of Europe. Other parts of the world are only sparsely populated, for example, northern Canada, northern Africa and much of Australia.

Why does population density vary from place to place?

There are several reasons why population density varies across the world. One of the main reasons is physical geography.

Figure 1.2 is a satellite image of the world. See how the green areas (indicating crops, grassland and forests) match the areas of highest population density on Figure 1.1. These

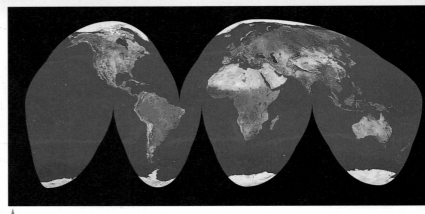

▲ *1.2 This satellite view of the world has been made up from different views of the earth*

areas are good for farming and, therefore, attractive to people. In contrast, the sandy brown areas on Figure 1.2 are deserts, such as the Sahara in Africa. Deserts have low population densities because the land is very dry and cannot support many people. Notice that the white areas (ice and snow) have very low population densities, as do the mountain ranges, with their steep slopes and harsh climates.

Raw materials such as coal have encouraged high population densities, for example, in parts of northern Europe. The development of industry and the growth of towns and cities took place where the raw materials were available.

Trade and industrial growth has led to many coastal parts of the world becoming densely populated, for example, the coast of South America.

---

1 Study Figure 1.1 – world population density.

a Make a copy of Figure 1.1 on a blank outline map of the world.

b Copy and complete Table 1.3 which will act as a key. Locate each letter from the key on your map using Atlas Maps A and B (pages 10–11 and 12–13) to help you. The 'reasons' are presented in boxes in Figure 1.4. You need to select the right reason for each area listed in the table.

▼ *1.4 Reasons for population density*

Narrow fertile strip along the course of a river surrounded by desert.	Very harsh climate and steep slopes.

Industry based on coal and favourable land for farming. Trade based on early empires.

Mostly covered by an ice sheet.	Coastal area first settled by Europeans. Good trading links with the rest of the world.

Huge area of forest. Very hot and humid.	Good land for farming and a very rapidly growing population.

Dry barren land unsuitable for farming and difficult to live in.	Wealthy industrial islands with limited space, hence a high density.

1.3 World population distribution key ▼

Area of world	Reason for population density
High density	
A Eastern USA	
B NW Europe	
C River Nile, Egypt	
D India	
E Japan	
Low density	
F Greenland	
G Amazon basin	
H Sahara desert	
I Himalayas	

Case study: population distribution in China

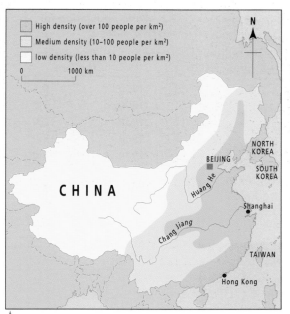

High density (over 100 people per km²)
Medium density (10–100 people per km²)
low density (less than 10 people per km²)

0   1000 km

N

CHINA

NORTH KOREA

BEIJING

SOUTH KOREA

Huang He

Shanghai

Chang Jiang

TAIWAN

Hong Kong

▲ *1.5 Population distribution in China*

The distribution of population in China is very uneven (Figure 1.5). The highest density is in the east and the lowest values are in the far west of the country. Eastern China has the highest population density because:

1 The wide river floodplains (e.g. Chang Jiang) and the extensive deltas provide fertile farmland (Photo 1.6).

2 Many large cities have developed on the coast as trading centres.

3 The mild and humid climate is well-suited to the development of settlement.

4 North east China has large industrial cities based on coal, iron ore and iron.

Western China is much more hostile and less suitable for human habitation (see Atlas Map A pages 10–11). The Tibetan Plateau is part of the Himalayan mountain range. Its cold winters and short growing season can only support small isolated villages. North Western China is part of the Gobi desert.

1.6 The Chang Jiang floodplain is very ▶
fertile and is good for farming

2 Study Figure 1.5.

a Make a copy of the Figure 1.5 on a blank outline map of China. Don't forget to include a key.

b In addition to the rivers already drawn, use Atlas Map A (pages 10–11) to help you locate and label the following physical features:
- the Tibetan Plateau
- the Himalayas
- the Gobi desert

c For each of the following regions of China, write a sentence or two giving reasons for its population density.
- eastern China
- north east China
- south west China
- north west China

3 Carry out your own study of population distribution in a country of your choice.

a Look carefully at Figure 1.1 (page 33) to select a country that has a range of population densities. Use Figure 1.1 to draw a simplified map of population distribution for your chosen country. Use Atlas Maps A and B (pages 10–11 and 12–13) to help you add labels to your map.

b Use Atlas Map A together with other maps and resources (atlases, textbooks, CD-Rom encyclopedias, etc) to attempt to explain the population distribution.

2 World population growth

The population of the world is about 6 billion. In the late 1990s it was estimated that over 80% lived in the economically developing world. China's population alone was 1.2 billion. At almost 1 billion, India's population was greater than the population of the whole of Europe.

The world's population is growing very rapidly, with 90 million extra mouths to feed each year. It is, however, only in the last few decades that the population of the world has risen so fast (see Figure 2.1). In 1900 the population was 1.5 billion and by 1950 it had only risen to 2.5 billion. Most growth has taken place in the second half of the 20th century and has been in the economically developing world.

2.2 World population for selected dates ▼

Date	Population (billion)
1650	0.5
1800	1.0
1930	2.0
1960	3.0
1974	4.0
1987	5.0
1998	6.0
2008	7.0*
2020	8.0*
2050	10.0*
* forecast	

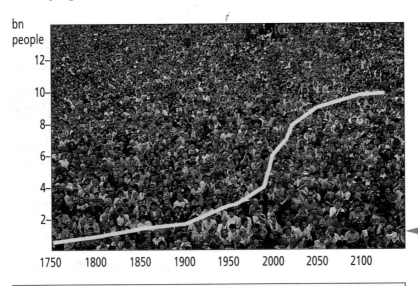

bn people (vertical axis: 2, 4, 6, 8, 10, 12; horizontal axis: 1750, 1800, 1850, 1900, 1950, 2000, 2050, 2100)

◀ **2.1 The world's population is continuing to grow quickly**

1 Present the information in Table 2.2 in the form of a line graph similar to Figure 2.1. Use the following axes for your graph:
- a horizontal scale of 1 cm = 50 years
- a vertical scale of 1 cm = 1 billion

a Use a pencil to plot each of the values in Table 2.2.

b Carefully join the points with a freehand line.

c Label the axes in ink.

d Write the following labels alongside your graph at the correct places:
- slow growth up to 1930
- very rapid growth from 1930–2050

e Now describe in your own words how the rate of growth of world population has changed since 1750.

f What challenges face the world in the light of the recent rapid increase in world population?

Patterns of population growth

Look at Figure 2.3. Notice that the highest rates of increase are in Africa, and in parts of the Middle East, South America and Asia. These are the regions that make up the economically developing world. The rest of the world has much lower rates of growth. A few countries (e.g. Germany, Bulgaria and Ukraine) even experienced a population decrease in the mid-1990s!

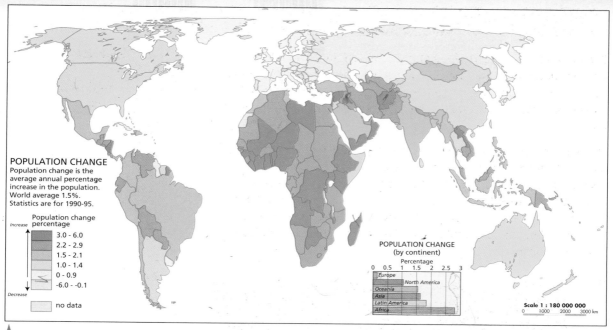

POPULATION CHANGE
Population change is the average annual percentage increase in the population. World average 1.5%. Statistics are for 1990-95.

Population change percentage

Increase

	3.0 - 6.0
	2.2 - 2.9
	1.5 - 2.1
	1.0 - 1.4
	0 - 0.9
	-6.0 - -0.1

Decrease

| | no data |

POPULATION CHANGE
(by continent)
Percentage
0   0.5   1   1.5   2   2.5   3
Europe
North America
Oceania
Asia
Latin America
Africa

Scale 1 : 180 000 000
0   1000   2000   3000 km

▲ 2.3 Patterns of population change

Why does population change?

There are two main factors that affect population change:

1 Birth rate. The number of live births per 1000 people.

2 Death rate. The number of deaths per 1000 people.

The difference between the birth rate and the death rate is called the **natural increase** (or natural decrease). The higher the natural increase, the faster the population growth. A high rate of natural increase will occur if the birth rate is high and the death rate is low. Look at Figure 2.4 to discover some reasons for high and low birth and death rates.

Birth rates

High

Lots of babies and young children die, so many have to be born in order that some will survive

Children are needed to work and earn money

Children are needed to support parents in old age

Some cultures and traditions value large families

Lack of family planning

Low

Greater wealth means that children are not needed to earn money

High survival rates (better hospitals, etc) mean that people don't need to have 'extra' children

Women choose to have children later in life

Family planning means people can decide the size of their families

Death rates

High

Famines

Lack of medicines, doctors and hospitals

Diseases caused by poor living conditions and diets

Low

Medicines, especially vaccinations, reduce disease and help people live longer

Better hospitals and living conditions mean fewer babies die

2.4 The causes of high and low birth and death rates ▶

Population change within a country can also be affected by a third factor, migration. **Migration** is the movement of people from one place to another. Some people choose to move to a country in search of a better quality of life. Others may be forced to move by war or natural disaster. As Figure 2.5 explains, it is a combination of natural increase and migration that causes population to change within a country or region.

Will the world population continue to rise?

Some people predict that in the 21st century world population growth will begin to slow down. By 2150 it might even have levelled out at about 11.5 billion. This is because advances in medicine and higher standards of living throughout the world will cause the death rate to fall. As this happens, people will begin to have fewer children and the birth rate will decline. With a low death rate and a low birth rate, world population growth will slow down.

▲ *2.5 The causes of population change*

2 Study Figure 2.3.

a Which continent has the highest rate of population increase?

b Which continent has the lowest rate of population increase?

c What is the rate of increase for the following countries
- Venezuela
- Libya
- New Zealand
- Italy
- Kenya
- Afghanistan?

d Use Atlas Map B (pages 12–13) to identify the country in northern Africa which has a population decrease.

e Use Atlas Map B (pages 12–13) to identify two European countries which have a population decrease.

3 For this activity you will need to make a copy of Table 2.6.

a Now complete the natural increase column. Australia has already been done for you.

b Use bars on a world map to show the natural increases for the ten countries. Use a scale of 1 cm = 10 per 1000 for the height of each bar. Make each bar 1 cm wide.

c Write a few sentences describing your map. Is there a difference in the natural increase between the 'rich' and 'poor' worlds?

2.6 Birth rates, death rates and natural increases (per 1000 population) for selected countries ▼

Country	Birth rate	Death rate	Natural increase
Australia	15	7	8
Brazil	25	7	
China	19	7	
Ethiopia	48	18	
India	29	10	
Iran	35	7	
Mexico	28	5	
Nigeria	45	15	
Sweden	14	11	
UK	13	11	

3 Population and resources

Resources are things that can be made use of. They include farmland and forests, rivers and oceans, metals, and sources of energy, such as coal and oil. Jobs, houses, food, clothes, and people can also be considered as resources. When the population of a country increases rapidly, its resources may be put under pressure.

In some parts of the world, population growth is putting a strain upon resources. There may not be enough food to go around or enough houses and jobs. People may starve or become homeless. However, population growth has sometimes been wrongly blamed for these

problems. Poor decisions by governments, war and natural disasters are often to blame.

In the future, population growth is expected to level off. Although finite resources (resources that are non-renewable) such as coal and oil, may eventually run out, technology will probably find alternatives. There will probably be enough food to feed the world's population, although its uneven distribution will cause shortages in some parts of the world. In addition, wars and natural disasters will continue to cause famine and disease.

1 Make a copy of Table 3.1 and complete the column describing some of the uses of the different resources shown.

a Can you suggest some other resources that are not shown in Figure 3.1?

▼ **3.1 Resources and their uses**

Resource	Uses
Farmland	
Freshwater lake	
River	
Forest	
Coal	
Animals	

2 How do you think a rapidly growing population might put pressure on the following resources :
- land for farming
- a freshwater lake
- a forest used for fuelwood?

Case study: Mauritius

Mauritius is a small island about the size of Buckinghamshire located in the Indian Ocean (see Atlas Map B pages 12–13). Much of the island is used for farming, with sugar cane being the most important crop. Mauritius has a tropical climate, which means that it is hot and humid throughout the year. Look at Figure 3.2 to discover more about the island of Mauritius.

The population of Mauritius grew slowly until the 1940s. Up until then, there had been a high death rate mainly due to the disease malaria. In the 1940s malaria was wiped out by, amongst other things, the introduction of medicines. This led to a rapid fall in the death rate.

The birth rate, however, remained high. This was largely because women were expected to marry when they were still teenagers. In marrying early, and with no family planning, large numbers of children were born.

▼ *3.2 Mauritius*

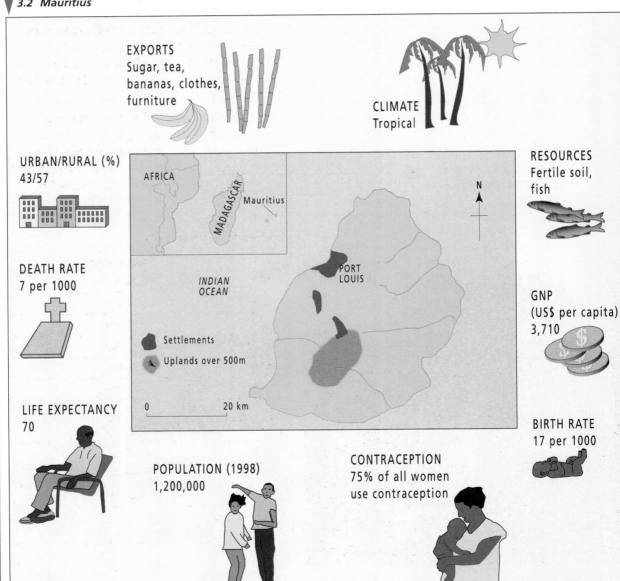

EXPORTS
Sugar, tea, bananas, clothes, furniture

CLIMATE
Tropical

URBAN/RURAL (%)
43/57

AFRICA

MADAGASCAR

Mauritius

RESOURCES
Fertile soil, fish

DEATH RATE
7 per 1000

INDIAN OCEAN

PORT LOUIS

N

GNP
(US$ per capita)
3,710

Settlements

Uplands over 500m

0   20 km

LIFE EXPECTANCY
70

POPULATION (1998)
1,200,000

CONTRACEPTION
75% of all women use contraception

BIRTH RATE
17 per 1000

The high birth rate and decreasing death rate resulted in a rapid surge in population. It seemed likely that the sugar cane industry alone would be unable to support the rapidly growing population. Something had to be done.

The government decided to try to slow down population growth and expand Mauritius's resources at the same time. A family-planning programme was introduced and women were encouraged to marry later. Schooling had to be paid for, which made children more expensive to bring up. The result of these measures was to reduce family sizes and slow down the speed of population growth.

The government also decided to encourage more tourism on the island (see Photo 3.3) to create jobs and bring in more money. As a result, many local people have benefited and standards of living have increased.

Today Mauritius has a steady rate of population growth and most people enjoy a comfortable standard of living. In the future, the country will be able to support its population.

▲ **3.3 The growth of tourism has meant a higher standard of living for people in Mauritius**

3 Mauritius forms an excellent case study of a country that has successfully coped with a rapidly rising population and a shortage of resources. Use the information in the case study to complete a small project about the island. Use the following headings in your project:

A **The geography of Mauritius.** Describe the island and its geography. Try to find out more about the country by using encyclopedias (including CD-ROMs like Encarta) and, if you have access, the Internet.

B **The population and resources problem.** Explain why the population began to grow so rapidly in the mid-20th century. What seemed likely to happen in the future if something wasn't done to solve the problem? Use the data in Table 3.4 to plot a population graph. Try to add some labels to describe the trends.

C **The solutions.** Describe how the government reduced the rate of population growth and increased resources. Does your population graph show signs of a slowing down of population growth? What does the future hold for Mauritius and its people?

▼ *3.4 Population in Mauritius*

Year	Population
1790	59 000
1900	370 000
1939	428 000
1959	631 200
1963	713 400
1972	800 000
1983	950 000
1992	1083 000
1998	1200 000
* 2010	1300 000
* 2025	1400 000
* predicted	

4 Migration

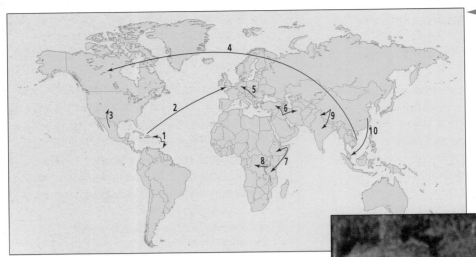

◀ *4.1 Recent worldwide migrations*

4.2 People are often forced to migrate because of wars or natural disasters like floods or volcanic eruptions ▼

Migration is the movement of people from place to place. Most migrations are voluntary, and involve people making a positive decision to set up their home in a new location. They may be changing job or simply wish to make a new start somewhere else.

Sometimes, however, people may be forced to move (see Figure 4.1 and Photo 4.2), due to war or a natural disaster, such as an earthquake or volcanic eruption. People that are forced to seek shelter in another country are called **refugees**. Worldwide there are estimated to be over 20 million refugees. An additional 25–30 million people have been made homeless in their own countries.

1 Study Figure 4.1.

a Make a copy of the migrations on to a blank world outline. Use a pencil first and then add colours.

b Select the correct description for each migration.
- Civil war drives Rwandan refugees to Zaire in 1994
- People flee to neighbouring Caribbean islands when Montserrat volcano erupts in 1997
- In the 1970s many Vietnamese 'boat people' flee communism and move to Hong Kong and Canada
- Mexicans seek a better life in the USA
- The 1991 Gulf War results in many Kurdish people moving from Iraq to Iran and Turkey
- In the 1960s West Indians move to the UK in search of jobs
- Tibetans cross the the Himalayas to India to escape Chinese-occupied Tibet
- Somalians move to Ethiopia and Tanzania due to war and famine in the 1980s
- Yugoslavians flee to Germany following civil war in the 1990s.
- People move to Malaysia to escape the famine in China in the 1960s

2 Look carefully at the Photo 4.2.

a Describe the hardships being faced by the people involved in the migrations

b Imagine that you were suddenly forced to leave your home. What possessions would you take and why?

Case study: the Kosovan refugee crisis 1999

Throughout most of the 1990s conflict has raged in the Balkans region of south-eastern Europe (Figure 4.3). The former Yugoslavia was made up of six republics. Four of them broke away in 1991/2 to form the countries of Bosnia-Herzegovina, Croatia, Macedonia and Slovenia (see Figure 4.3). Serbia and Montenegro formed a new, smaller Yugoslavia in 1992.

A large number of people of Albanian origin had become settled in the southern Yugoslav province of Kosovo (see Figure 4.3). In 1998, the Kosovo Liberation Army (KLA) announced its intention to unify the province with neighbouring Albania. The Serbian army was ordered in to quell the uprising. It soon became clear that the Yugoslav president Slobadan Milosevic was intent on clearing the province of all ethnic Albanians. This policy is known as **ethnic cleansing**.

▲ **4.3 The split of Yugoslavia**

In early 1999 over 750,000 Kosovan Albanians fled from their homes in fear of their lives. They moved towards the neighbouring countries of Albania and Macedonia.

Massive tent cities (refugee camps) were established in the neighbouring countries, often administered by the United Nations High Commission for Refugees (UNHCR). Conditions were very cramped and there were some shortages of food, water and medical equipment. Many countries ran appeals to raise aid.

In March 1999, the North Atlantic Treaty Organisation (NATO) decided to take military action in an attempt to stop the Serbian government continuing to force Kosovans from their homes. Later in 1999, the Kosovans began to return to their homeland to rebuild their shattered lives.

▲ **4.4 Kosovan refugees queueing to get over the border**

3 Study the section about the Kosovan refugees.

a What is a refugee?

b What is meant by the term ethnic cleansing and how was it responsible for the Kosovan crisis?

c Study Photo 4.4. What do you think conditions would have been like for refugees?

4 Discuss whether it was right for NATO to respond to the crisis with military action.

Web Search

Use the Internet to update the Kosovan refugee crisis. Try the United Nations High Commission for Refugees (UNHCR).

Tectonic hazards

The major features of the earth's surfaces such as the high mountain ranges and the deep sea trenches owe their existence to powerful, natural tectonic forces. These massive forces, which originate far below the surface of the earth, come to our attention when earthquakes and volcanic eruptions strike, often with disastrous effects.

1 Tectonic hazards in Colombia

The country of Colombia in South America suffers frequent small earthquakes and minor volcanic eruptions. However, in the space of just 14 years, two tragic events have struck with awesome power and consequences (Figure 1.1).

Earthquake 1999

On 25 January 1999 at 1.09 pm a strong earthquake rumbled through the mountain cities of Armenia and Pereira (Figure 1.1) . Within just a few seconds buildings collapsed and many people were killed or injured. It is estimated that over 1,000 people were killed by the earthquake, and hundreds of thousands were left homeless.

Scientists use the **Richter Scale** to measure the strength of an earthquake. Each point on the Richter Scale represents a x30 increase in energy. The Colombian earthquake measured 6.0.

1.1 Recent natural disasters in Colombia

COLOMBIAN EARTHQUAKE KILLS 1000: DEATH TOLL EXPECTED TO CLIMB

At least 1,000 people are dead, thousands more injured, and tens of thousands homeless, following a powerful earthquake on Monday that levelled major portions of western Colombia.

In the hard-hit city of Armenia, rescue workers scrambled to free people trapped in the rubble of collapsed buildings. City residents clawed at the tangled concrete and steel cables with shovels, sticks, and hands to reach the victims. The deputy fire chief of Armenia said that at least 1,000 people were dead, 'perhaps more than 2,000 in Armenia alone'. The hardest-hit cities were Armenia, Pereira, and Calarca. At least half of Armenia, which sits high in the Andes mountains, was devastated by the quake.

1.2 Many houses collapsed completely under the force of the earthquake in Armenia

1 Study Photo 1.2.

a Suggest some of the immediate effects of the earthquake.

b Work with a friend to suggest some of the longer-term problems (in the forthcoming weeks and months) that might have affected the people in the area.

2 Carry out an Internet search to find out about recent earthquakes. the BBC website is a good place to start.

An observer describes the devastation after the volcano ▶

Volcano 1985

On 13 November 1985 shortly after 9 pm, the 5200m high volcano Nevado del Ruiz erupted (Figure 1.1). The massive eruption sent ash and burning rocks over 8,000 metres into the air. The many glaciers on the volcano side melted, sending torrents of water down the river valley. When the ash fell to ground it became mixed with the water to form deadly mudflows called **lahars**. One of these lahars tore into the town of Armero burying its 22,000 inhabitants in up to 8m of mud (Figure 1.3). In total, an estimated 25,000 people were killed by this single volcanic eruption, making it the 4th most deadly eruption of all time.

It was difficult to reach (Armero) for all the rivers were swollen and many bridges were down. There are hundreds of corpses floating down the rivers and a suffocating smell of sulphur in the air. It has to be one of the world's biggest mass graves. It looks like a beach at low tide, just mud and driftwood. One 12-year-old girl, trapped in the mud from the waist down, said that she was standing on the corpses of her father and aunt.

1.3 *People in Armero were buried alive by a lahar following the eruption of Nevada del Ruiz.*

What caused the disasters?

Look back to Figure 1.1 and find the location of the earthquake and the volcanic eruption. Notice that they occurred very close to one another. Perhaps the two events are connected? Notice also that they occurred in the Andes mountains. Could there be a link?

3 Study Figure 1.3.

a Make a simple sketch of Figure 1.3 to show what happened when Nevado del Ruiz erupted.

b What are lahars?

c Why did the site of Armero make it vulnerable to a lahar?

d The lahar hit Armero at night. Do you think the death toll might have been different had it hit during the day? Explain your answer.

2 Global tectonics

The theory of **plate tectonics** states that the outermost layer of the earth is divided into a number of huge slabs some 100 km thick. Each slab is called a **plate**.

The plates rest on a layer in the upper mantle (see Figure 2.1) that is slightly mobile, allowing each plate to move in relation to its neighbour. The reason why the plates move at all is because there are currents of heat moving deep within the

2.1 The structure of the Earth ▶

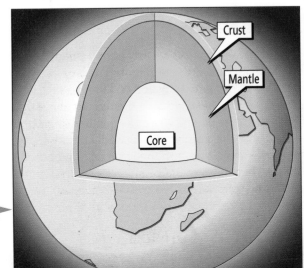

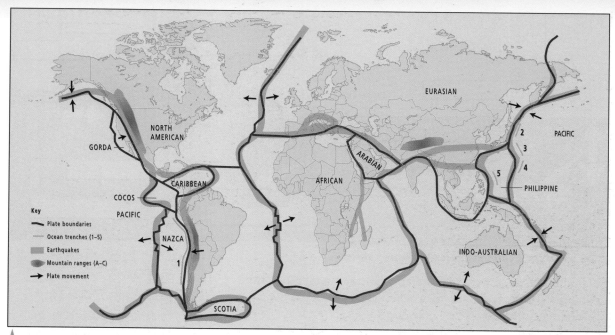

▲ **2.2 The worldwide distribution of earthquakes, ocean trenches and mountain belts**

mantle. It is hard to imagine what is happening, but if you have seen custard or porridge cooking, you may have seen the effects of rising heat cracking and then spreading the skin on the surface

Now look at Figure 2.2. It shows the distribution of earthquakes around the world. Notice that they form a number of clear linear zones. Scientists have used this pattern of earthquakes to mark the edges of the major plates.

Notice that some plate margins have a great deal of earthquake activity, such as the boundary of the Nazca and the South American plates. Some earthquakes do occur away from plate margins. There are a number of possible causes of mid-plate earthquakes, including underground mining.

Now look at Figure 2.3 which shows what is happening beneath the Andes mountains in Colombia. Notice that there are two plates moving towards one other. See how one plate is diving beneath the other. As the Nazca plate dives beneath the South American plate, stresses build as the slabs of rock try to slide past each other. When the force of the moving plates overcomes friction, the resultant jolt causes an earthquake to occur. The point where the jolt

happens is called the **focus**. The point on the surface immediately above the focus is called the **epicentre**.

1 Study Figure 2.2. You will need to refer to Atlas Map A (pages 10–11) to help you with some of the following activities.

a Identify the names of the ocean trenches labelled 1–5 on Figure 2.2.

b Which of the five trenches is the deepest and how deep is it?

c Discover the names of the mountain ranges labelled A–C on Figure 2.2.

d The Marianas Trench is found at the margin of which two plates?

e Which two plates are responsible for the formation of the Himalayas?

f An earthquake has occurred in the Red Sea. Which two plates are likely to be responsible?

g Why are people living in New Zealand more likely to experience an earthquake than people living in neighbouring Australia?

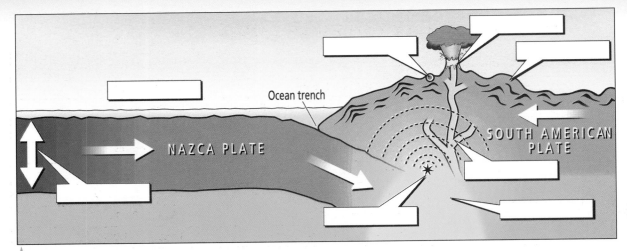

Ocean trench

NAZCA PLATE

SOUTH AMERICAN PLATE

▲ 2.3 How the Colombian disasters were caused

Friction and heat at the plate margin also causes melting of the diving plate to form molten rock called **magma**. The magma rises towards the surface to create volcanic eruptions such as the one at Nevado del Ruiz. As the two plates move towards each other, the rocks become folded and buckled upwards to form the Andes mountains.

Plate tectonics helps to explain other features of the Earth's surface. Ocean trenches are huge gashes in the ocean floor up to 10 km deep. They occur where one plate dives beneath another, such as off the coast of Colombia (see Figure 2.3). Many of the world's mountain ranges mark the edges of plates too (see Figure 2.2). They form when two plates collide and force the rocks upwards (see Figure 2.3). This process causes the rocks to be buckled or folded (Photo 2.4).

In the following two sections we will look at two countries on, or very close to, active plate margins.

▼ 2.4 Rocks can be folded by pressure

2 Study Figure 2.3.

a Make a copy of Figure 2.3.

b Complete the empty boxes by choosing the correct labels from the following list:
- focus of earthquake
- Andes mountains
- plate 100 km thick
- epicentre of 1999 earthquake
- rising magma
- Pacific Ocean
- Nevado del Ruiz volcano
- magma

c Complete your diagram by using colours and giving it a title.

3 Study Figure 2.3.

a What is a plate?

b What causes the plates to move in relation to each other?

c Explain how the Colombian earthquake of 1999 was caused. Use the terms focus and epicentre in your explanation.

d How is magma formed beneath the Andes mountains?

e Try to suggest in your own words why it is not simply a coincidence that the earthquake, volcano and mountain range all occur together.

4 For this activity you will need a blank outline map of the world. Study Table 2.5.

▼ *2.5 Volcanic eruptions 1998–1999*

Jan	1998	Sauura-Jima, Japan	31.58N 130.67E
Feb	1998	Rincon de la Vieja, Costa Rica	10.20N 85.50W
March	1998	Reunion, Indian Ocean	21.23S 55.71E
April	1998	Karymsky, Kamchatka, Russia	54.0N 159.5E
June	1998	Korovin, Alaska	52.38N 174.15W
July	1998	Mt St Helens, USA	46.20N 122.18W
July	1998	Papandayan, Java, Indonesia	7.32S 107.73E
July	1998	Iwate-san, Honshu, Japan	39.85N 141.00E
Sept	1998	Stromboli, Italy	38.8N 15.2E
Sept	1998	Pacaya, Guatemala	14.4N 90.6W
Oct	1998	Manam, Papua New Guinea	4.1S 145.0E
Nov	1998	Cerro Negro, Nicaragua	12.5N 86.7W
Dec	1998	Popocatepetl, Mexico	19.0N 98.6W
Dec	1998	Grimsvotn, Iceland	64.5N 17.36W
Jan	1999	Azores, S. Atlantic	38.7N 27.3W
Jan	1999	White Island, New Zealand	37.52S 177.18E
Jan	1999	Guagua Pinhincha, Ecuador	0.17S 78.60W
Jan	1999	Montserrat, W. Indies	16.7N 62.2W

a Use Atlas Map B (pages 12–13) to help you locate the volcanoes listed in Table 2.5. Locate each volcano with a symbol of your choice, for example, a volcano shape.

b Now mark on to your map the plates using Figure 2.2. Use pencil first and then use a colour to show the margins clearly.

c Complete your map by naming the volcanoes and the plates. Give your map a title.

d Do the volcanoes coincide with the plate margins?

e Is this what you expected? Why?

Web Search

There is a tremendous amount of information available on the Internet about volcanoes and earthquakes, particularly good for project work. Find out about recent earthquakes or volcanic eruptions by looking at the following American web sites:

Volcano World at www.volcano.und.nodak.edu/vw html

National Earthquake Information Center at www.neic.cr.usgs.gov/

You will also find many links to infomation in countries outside the United States which are well worth visiting.

Carry out a study of a volcano of your choice. Try to find out about the nature of its eruptions and the effect of its eruptions on people. See if you can discover some benefits to people who live close to the volcano. Include a map to show the volcano's location and attempt to show the plates in the area.

3 Living with volcanoes in Iceland

Iceland is sometimes known as the 'land of fire and ice'. This is because it has a great deal of volcanic activity and has several ice caps and glaciers. Look at Figure 3.1. The areas shaded white are covered by ice. Vatnajokull in the south-east is the largest ice cap in Europe. The mountain peaks of Hekla and Grimsvotn are two examples of Iceland's many volcanoes, the latter being beneath the Vatnajokull ice cap!

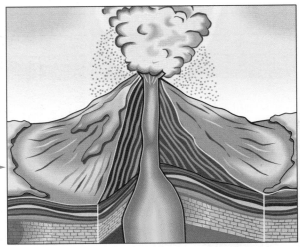

3.1 Iceland showing the mid-Atlantic ridge

Volcanic eruptions on Iceland

It is hardly surprising that Iceland has several active volcanoes because it sits astride a plate margin, called the **mid-Atlantic Ridge** (Figure 3.1). Here molten magma escapes to the surface as the two plates move apart. It cools down to form the rocks that make up the island. In fact, Iceland is still growing. In 1963/1964 undersea eruptions led to the formation of a new island just off the south coast of Iceland. It was named Surtsey. Can you find it on Figure 3.1?

3.2 An erupting cone volcano ▶

3.3 During a fissure eruption like this in Krafla, Iceland, lava spills out of a crack in the earth's surface ▼

1 Study Figure 3.1.

a Which is the nearest mainland settlement to the island of Surtsey?

b What is the highest peak on Iceland?

c You have just landed at Keflavik International Airport.
  ● How far do you have to travel to reach the Icelandic capital Reykjavik?
  ● In what direction do you have to travel?

There are two sorts of volcanic eruption on Iceland. The first is a central vent eruption, where magma reaches the surface through a single hole (Figure 3.2). These eruptions produce large amounts of red-hot **lava** (magma that has reached the surface) together with ash and rocks blasted high into the air. They form the typical volcano shape. The second type of eruption involves a fissure (long crack) (see Photo 3.3). Rather than forming a volcano, fissure eruptions tend to form an extensive flat surface called a **plateau**.

Monitoring volcanoes

The volcanoes on Iceland are very carefully monitored by scientists on the ground. They study patterns of small earthquakes, look for slight bulges in the sides of volcanoes and monitor levels of gases in craters. Maps identify possible danger areas and people are evacuated if an eruption is likely. High above the Earth, satellites look at volcanoes for minute increases in temperature which could warn of a possible eruption.

2 Study Figure 3.1 and the text.

a Why does Iceland have so many volcanoes?

b Which volcanic eruption formed a new island in 1963/4?

c How does a central vent eruption differ from a fissure eruption?

3 Study Figure 3.2.

a Make a large copy of Figure 3.2 using colours to make your diagram clear and attractive.

b Write the following labels in their correct places:
- magma rising to the surface
- cloud of ash and rocks
- lava flowing down volcano
- layers of ash and lava
- volcano
- ash falling to the ground

3.4 The formation of hot water by geothermal energy ▽

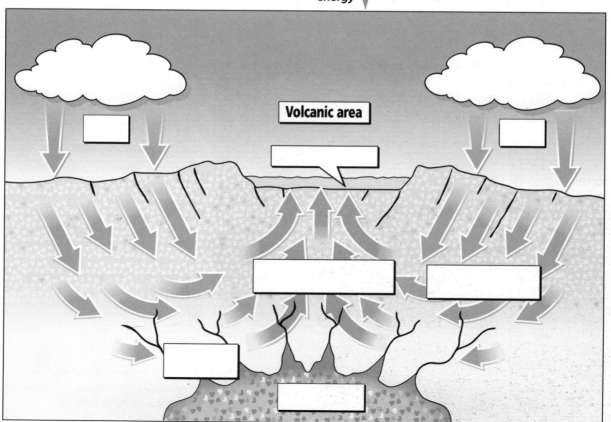

Volcanic area

The benefits of volcanic activity

The people of Iceland benefit in many ways from living on an active plate margin.

- About 44% of Iceland's total energy comes from **geothermal energy** where boiling underground water, heated by the hot rocks deep below the surface, produces stream which can be used to generate electricity.

- Some 85% of all homes in Iceland are heated by this natural hot water which is piped to houses. Most of Reykjavik's hot water comes from the Nesjavellir geothermal plant some 35 km away where the natural heat from the Earth is used to heat freshwater from a nearby lake.

- Over 120 mostly open-air swimming pools are heated by the naturally occuring hot water.

3.5 The Blue Lagoon is an open-air swimming pool which is heated by geothermal energy

Swimming and bathing are extremely popular pastimes in Iceland whatever the weather.

- Spent water from the heating of houses is used to melt snow on pavements and in car parks.

- Greenhouses producing tomatoes, cucumbers and flowers are heated using geothermal energy.

- The volcanic rocks provide building materials and valuable minerals, and weather down to produce fertile soils for farming.

- Many tourists are attracted to Iceland's geothermal sites, for example, to see the geysir at Geysir.

3.6 Fruit and vegetables from warmer climates can be grown in greenhouses heated by geothermal energy

4 Study Figure 3.4 and the section 'The benefits of volcanic activity'.

a Make a copy of Figure 3.4 which describes how natural hot water occurs in Iceland. Add the following labels in their correct places:
- precipitation
- cold water soaks into the rocks
- magma: source of underground volcanic heat
- water is heated up
- hot water and steam escapes to the surface
- pool of hot water

b Write a couple of sentences describing how precipitation falling on the ground can become rising hot water.

c What is geothermal energy and why is it an example of a renewable form of energy?

5 Make a copy of the temperature line shown in Figure 3.7. Use a scale of 1cm = 100° C.

a Write alongside the line at the correct place each of the following uses of hot water:
- 140°C canning food
- 130°C sugar-refining
- 100°C washing and drying wool
- 80°C space heating of houses and greenhouses
- 50°C mushroom-growing
- 30°C swimming pools
- 25°C snow-melting
- 20°C fish-farming

b Several geothermal plants use the hottest water first for electricity generation. As it cools it is then used for central (space) heating. Then the water is used for swimming pools and snow melting. This is described as a "cascade". Does your diagram support this idea?

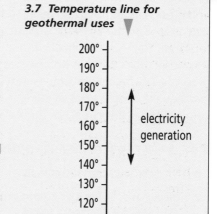

3.7 Temperature line for geothermal uses

electricity generation

---

4 Living with earthquakes in Japan

Japan experiences more earthquakes than any other country in the world. Each year, the country is rocked by between 7,000 and 8,000 earthquakes. The vast majority are very minor. However, about 1,500 are strong enough to be felt by people, and a few cause damage to buildings and trigger landslides.

Why does Japan have so many earthquakes?

The reason why there are so many earthquakes in Japan is because the country lies along a complex and active plate margin (see Figure 4.1). There are in fact four major plates that meet in the Japan area, and it is the jerky slippage between them that causes the earthquakes.

Japan's worst earthquake struck Tokyo in 1923 (Figure 4.1). About 140,000 people were killed and nearly 600,000 homes were completely destroyed by the 8.3 magnitude earthquake. In terms of loss of life, it is the ninth most severe earthquake ever to occur in the world.

To understand more about the effects of earthquakes in Japan, let's take a closer look at one of the most recent earthquakes.

The Kobe earthquake, 1995

In 1995 the industrial city of Kobe (Figure 4.1) was devastated by an earthquake measuring 7.2 on the Richter scale. The scale of destruction was awesome. Over 6,000 people were killed and

35,000 injured. Some 300,000 people were made homeless as buildings collapsed. Over 300 fires raged through the city as gas pipes were ruptured. Some of the most dramatic damage was done to sections of Kobe's motorways (Photo 4.3) which were supposed to be 'earthquake proof'! Look at Table 4.2 to discover some of the other effects of the Kobe earthquake.

▼ **4.2 Some effects of the Kobe earthquake, 1995**

- 1 million households had no water
- thousands of bodies lay in schools and sports centres as there was a shortage of coffins
- the Port of Kobe was badly hit with over 90% of its ships' berths destroyed
- many people suffered financial loss as only 3% of people were insured
- many kilometres of roads and railways were damaged
- electricity and gas networks were seriously disrupted
- nearly US$100 billion worth of damage was caused
- a large number of people became unemployed as damaged industries relocated outside Kobe

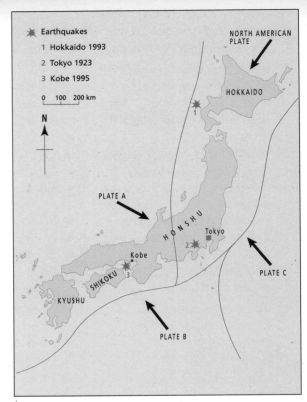

▲ **4.1 Earthquakes and plate margins in Japan**

▼ **4.3 Sections of the main highway in Kobe collapsed**

Few of us have had the experience of being in an earthquake, but it is possible for us to imagine how terrifying it must be. Yasuyo Morita, aged 17, posted her account of the earthquake on the Internet (Figure 4.4).

---

1 Read Yasuyo's account of the earthquake (Figure 4.4). Her account was posted on the Internet. Imagine that she had asked people to e-mail her. Write a few sentences responding to her account. Take time to think what to say. It is not an easy task.

2 Study Table 4.2 and the section about the Kobe earthquake.

a Draw up two lists to identify the short-term (immediate) effects of the earthquake and the longer-term effects.

b Which short-term effect do you think caused the greatest hardship to the survivors and why?

c Which of the long-term effects do you think is most significant and why?

How can the earthquake hazard be reduced in the future?

Scientists are still trying to find a way to predict earthquakes reliably. Sometimes, just before a large earthquake occurs, there are warning signs. These include slight rises or falls in the land, changes in underground water levels and even strange animal behaviour. However, no foolproof method yet exists. Most earthquakes happen suddenly without any warning at all.

People who live in areas prone to earthquakes, such as in Japan and the west coast of the USA, can prepare themselves by becoming educated about what to do when an earthquake happens. In Japan, earthquake drills are as common as fire drills are in British schools. City authorities can plan for new buildings and bridges to be built to cope with the shaking that takes place during an earthquake (Figure 4.5). Provision can be made for the storage of emergency supplies such as food, water, medicines and shelter, all of which are needed after an earthquake.

▼ 4.4 *Yasuyo Morita (17 years old)*

At the time I was sleeping. First I thought my mother was waking me up, but I knew from her scream – it is an earthquake. I didn't know what to do in the dark. The stairs are destroyed, so I went down using a ladder, with bare feet, wearing pyjamas. I couldn't stop my tears because of the darkness and coldness. I was in a panic.

There are a lot of wooden houses in my neighbourhood. Now they are destroyed without pity. Soon it got lighter and I could see my surroundings. Some went mad. I went to hospital with my grandmother who was rescued from a heap of rubble. Her injury was not serious compared with others. My grandmother's house and my grandfather's house, both are burnt down. Now I live in one of the refuges and I get scared during the night. I want to see Kobe rebuilt again.

▲ 4.5 *Buildings can be built to resist earthquakes*

Tsunamis are huge sea waves triggered by earthquakes. They can be up to 10 metres high. They are rather easier to predict than the earthquakes that trigger them. Since 1952, the Japanese Meteorological Agency has monitored the seas around Japan. Within 20 minutes of an earthquake occurring, the Agency can issue warnings to coastal areas at risk from these huge waves and people can be moved to higher ground. The warnings, issued over the radio and on the television, have saved thousands of lives. Look at Figure 4.6 to discover some other ways of reducing the tsunami hazard.

3 Study Figure 4.5.

a Make a careful copy of Figure 4.5.

b Add the following labels in their correct places:
- automatic shutters come down over windows
- deep and firm building foundations
- rubber shock absorbers beneath the building
- rolling weights on the roof to counteract the shock waves
- open areas for pedestrians to assemble
- identification number on the roof visible to helicopters

c Why do you think automatic shutters that come down over windows is a good idea?

d Suggest why identification numbers are displayed on the roofs of buildings?

e Many buildings in Japanese cities are built to withstand shaking. Why do you think similar designs are less common in LEDCs?

4 Study Figure 4.6. Describe with the help of simple sketches how a coastline could be protected from a tsunami.

▼ 4.6 Reducing the tsunami hazard

- If you are at the beach, or near the ocean, and you feel the earth shake, move immediately to higher ground. DO NOT wait for a tsunami warning to be announced. Stay away from rivers and streams which are near the ocean
- If you live in a tsunami evacuation zone and you feel the earth shake, or hear a tsunami warning, you should make sure that your whole family evacuates the house. Move in an orderly, calm and safe manner to the evacuation site (on higher ground). Follow the advice of the emergency authorities.

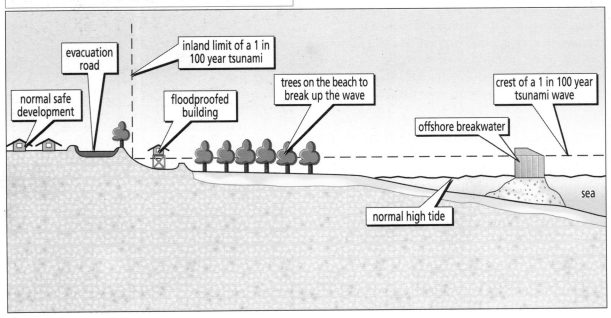

Tourism

Tourism is now one of the largest industries in the world. Each year in the 1990s about 500 million people (about 8 times the population of the UK) visited a foreign country. Tourism brings huge amounts of money to countries and creates many jobs. However, tourism also brings problems such as environmental damage, crime, and exploitation of local people.

1 The growth of tourism

A tourist is defined as a person who spends at least one night away from home. During the summer holidays, most of us become tourists when we go camping, stay with friends or go to a foreign country.

1.1 Tourists ▶

1.2 Holiday destinations for a class of year 9 students ▼

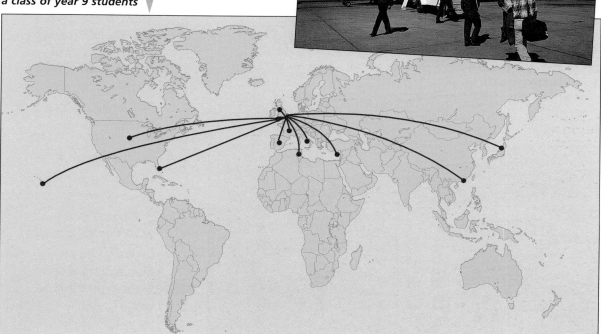

More and more people now travel abroad for their holidays (Photo 1.1). There are three main reasons for the growth in foreign holidays:

1 People have more money to spend than they used to and they can make use of loans from banks if they wish to.

2 Holidays are longer than they used to be. Most people can now have at least 4 or 5 weeks paid holiday a year.

3 Foreign travel has become cheaper and easier. Holiday companies provide all-inclusive package holidays and cut-price tickets.

Tourism winners and losers

Many countries encourage tourism. This is because tourists bring huge amounts of money into a country and many jobs are created to cater for the tourists. Hotels have to be built and lots of local people are employed to run and service them. Roads and airports are constructed and local farmers are encouraged to grow more food. Tourism has led to improvements in many people's quality of life, especially in the less economically developed world.

However, tourism has also brought problems. The local people may be paid very low wages, and crime and prostitution may be encouraged. Modern 'western' habits can sometimes conflict with traditional cultures. For example, in some countries the wearing of bikinis and even shorts can cause great offence.

Environmental damage is another serious problem. Minibuses full of camera-clicking tourists can upset wildlife and damage the countryside (Photo 1.4). Coastal habitats can be destroyed to make way for hotel development, and coral reefs in particular can be badly damaged by boat anchors and people walking on them.

1.4 Tourism brings money to a country, but can also have an environmental impact ▼

1 Study Figure 1.2. Now discover where your class went on holiday last summer. Use Atlas Map B (pages 12–13) to plot the locations on a blank outline map of the world.

2 Write a couple of sentences to explain why foreign tourism has grown so fast in recent years.

3 Study Table 1.3.

a Use Atlas Map B (pages 12–13) to plot the location of the places listed in Table 1.3.

▼ *1.3 Flight deals*

Melbourne	£493
Perth	£507
Hong Kong	£317
Singapore	£368
Los Angeles	£268
Montreal	£239
Toronto	£239
Buenos Aires	£426

b Draw coloured lines linking the UK to the places you have plotted using the key below:

£201–£300	orange
£301–£400	red
£401–£500	brown
£501+	black

Try to explain any pattern you observe.

4 Now study Photo 1.4.

a What advantages do you think tourism can bring to a country?

b In what ways is the environment being damaged?

c Can you suggest any additional problems that tourism might bring to a country?

2 Ecotourism

Tourism can have serious effects on the environment and on the lives of local people. Look at Figure 2.1 to discover some negative effects that have resulted from tourism in different parts of the world.

Recently more and more tourists wish to experience nature and learn about the natural world rather than being herded into high-rise hotels in artificial tourist resorts.

This kind of 'natural' tourism, called **ecotourism**, often involves small groups of people and does not harm the environment. It also respects the beliefs and ways of life of local people. It is a form of **sustainable tourism** because it ensures that the resources are not damaged for future generations.

1 Study Figure 2.1.

a Locate and draw the areas listed in Table 2.1 onto a blank outline map of the world. Use Atlas Map B (pages 12–13) to help you.

b Use a different colour to shade each area. Add labels to describe the negative effects that tourism is bringing to each area.

2 Describe in your own words what is meant by the term ecotourism.

3 Study the information about Rara Avis on page 60.

a What is the climate like at Rara Avis?

b A great deal of wildlife can be seen in the rainforest at Rara Avis. What would you be most interested to see and why?

c Families are allowed to visit Rara Avis. Is it the kind of holiday that you would like your family to go on? Give reasons for your answer.

4 How does the Rara Avis project benefit the following:
- tourists
- the local people
- the natural environment?

a) The Swiss Alps: Forests cut down to create ski runs and resorts. Avalanches more likely.

b) Mallorca: Coastal developments damage the natural landscape and destroy farmland.

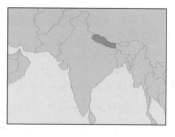

c) The Nepalese Foothills: Trekkers damage fragile ecosystems, cause footpath erosion and leave litter.

d) The Caribbean: Marinas, harbours and resort developments cause destruction to swamp ecosystems.

e) Kenya: Tourist minibuses on safari reduce vegetation cover and increase soil erosion. Animals are upset by noise.

2.1 Negative effects of tourism on the environment

Case study: the Rara Avis project in Costa Rica

Costa Rica is described as being one of the healthiest, safest and most peaceful countries in the world. It lies in Central America (see Atlas Map B, pages 12–13), has a tropical climate and is about 2/3 the size of Scotland. Costa Rica has a population of about 3 million people and its capital city, San Jose, has about the same population as Newcastle-upon-Tyne. Costa Rica is well known for its natural beauty (see Figure 2.2b) and it has become a very popular tourist destination in recent years.

2.2a) *Many species of parrot live in the rainforest*

Rara Avis is set in the heart of Costa Rica's rainforest (see Photo 2.2b) about 50 km north of San Jose. Only 20% of the original rainforest now remains following widespread destruction to make way for cattle ranching. Much of what is left is now protected in the form of National Parks.

Rara Avis is a small forest village established by the government in 1983 to form a base for scientists and tourists wishing to learn more about the rainforest. Visitors can view toucans breakfasting in the treetops, pick up arrow-poison frogs and watch the bats at night. Up to 60 people can be accommodated in two lodges.

Local people are involved in the project. In earning money from the rainforest, they do not need to cut down trees to create more land for their cattle to graze. Tourism provides them with an additional source of income.

Rara Avis is an excellent example of sustainable tourism. It shows how tourism can benefit the tourist, the local people and the natural environment without doing any damage.

At 700 meters (2000ft) above sea level, the climate stays cool and comfortable all year round (77^0 F or 25^0C). There is a lot of rain (it's a rainforest), but mosquitoes are not a problem.

Over 340 species of birds have been found at Rara Avis, including sunbitterns, umbrella-birds, great green macaws, parrots and toucans. There is a good chance to see monkeys, anteaters, or coatimundis if you walk silently through the forest, or to spot the tracks of tapirs and jungle cats. There are more kinds of plants, butterflies and birds than in all of Europe.

2.2b) *The rainforest attracts many tourists to Costa Rica*

3 Tourism in Egypt

Egypt is one of the most popular tourist destinations in the world. It is well known for its many ancient sites such as the Pyramids, the Valley of the Kings and the Sphynx (Photo 3.1c). Some people choose to take a cruise on the River Nile while others opt for a beach holiday alongside the Red Sea (Photo 3.1b).

"Ancient wonders, modern comforts and the timeless majesty of the Nile; Egypt impresses holiday-makers from every angle. Wooden craft with single curling sails tack between the banks, bullocks work in the fields and spindly pumps draw water for irrigation. Children run along the banks and men and women stoop over their work in the fields. Beneath the blazing desert sun, Egypt ignites the imagination as few other countries do."

3.1a) Extract from Thomson's 'Faraway Shores' brochure 1999

3.1c) The pyramids are a popular tourist attraction ▼

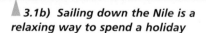

3.1b) Sailing down the Nile is a relaxing way to spend a holiday

1 Look at the information in Figure 3.1a).

a What attracts tourists to Egypt?

b Either
- If you have been to Egypt describe why you went there, what you saw and what you thought about your visit.

Or
- If you have not visited Egypt, would you like to go there on holiday? Give reasons for your answer.

TOURISM

3.2 Climate data for Luxor and London

	J	F	M	A	M	J	J	A	S	O	N	D
Luxor's average daily temperature (°C)	23	26	31	36	39	42	41	41	39	37	31	25
London's average daily temperature (°C)	6	7	10	13	17	20	22	21	19	14	10	7
Luxor's average monthly rainfall (mm)	0	0	0	0	0	0	0	0	0	0	0	0
Luxor's average daily sunshine (hours)	9	10	10	11	12	12	12	12	11	10	9	9

The climate of Egypt encourages people to visit because for much of the year it is hot and sunny. This is hardly surprising because most of Egypt is a desert with only the River Nile creating a corridor of human settlement. Look at Table 3.2. Notice that the temperatures are far higher in Luxor than in London. See how little rain falls too.

Tourism has grown faster than any other sector of the economy. Over 260,000 people are employed in the tourism industry working in hotels, shops or at the main tourist sites. In addition, thousands more local people make and sell souvenirs, provide food or act as guides. The number of shops and restaurants has more than doubled since the early 1980s. New roads have been built and services such as water and sanitation have been improved.

2 Look at the climate data in Table 3.2.

a Use the information in Table 3.2 to plot a bar chart to compare temperatures in Luxor with those of London. Look at Figure 3.3 to see how to plot the data so that it can be compared.

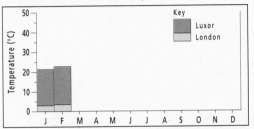

3.3 Temperature chart for Luxor and London

b Write a few sentences comparing the temperatures of the two places.

c Use your completed graph together with other information in Table 3.2 to suggest why the climate of Luxor encourages tourists to visit.

3.4 Where tourists visiting Egypt come from (1997)

Saudi Arabia	210,000
Libya	180,000
Kuwait	70,000
Jordan	70,000
France	260,000
Germany	440,000
UK	334,000
Italy	390,000
Switzerland	110,000
Scandinavia	60,000
Austria	60,000
Japan	90,000
USA	180,000
Russian Federation	120,000

3 Study the information in Table 3.4. Produce a flow map to show the origins of tourists to Egypt. To do this you will need an outline map of the world. Work in pencil first.

a Locate each country listed in Table 3.4 using Atlas Map B (pages 12–13) to help you.

b Draw an arrow from each country to Egypt to show the flow of tourists. Each arrow should be drawn so that its width indicates how many tourists travelled. You will need to work out a scale, e.g. 1cm = 200,000 people. Your completed map will have several arrows of different thickness.

c Use a colour to shade the arrows and write the names of the countries on the map or in a key.

d Give your map a title.

e Write a few sentences about your map
- where do most tourists come from?
- do most tourists come from countries close to Egypt?

Try to give some reasons for the patterns you observe.

Diving in Egypt

The town of El Qusei is situated on the west shore of the Red Sea. The Red Sea is a paradise for divers and many people travel to places like El Quseir to enjoy diving holidays. The great attraction for tourists, in addition to the hot, sunny weather, is the large expanse of coral reef found along the coast. The reef is teeming with life, and many people take short courses in snorkelling or scuba-diving to enable them to swim among the fish (Photo 3.5).

In addition to underwater activities, tourists can take part in jet skiing, para sailing, water skiing and windsurfing. On dry land, hotels offer swimming pools, beaches and the opportunity to take desert safaris.

There is huge potential for tourism along Egypt's 1000 km Red Sea coastline, and the government is encouraging several large developments. These developments will include 5-star hotels, tourist villages, and marinas.

In the past, developments have caused damage to the environment. Some stretches of coral were destroyed to make way for sandy beaches, and other parts of the reef became polluted. Short-term profit was leading to long-term damage of the environment. This is an excellent example of unsustainable tourism.

In 1991 the Tourism Development Authority was set up to oversee new developments. It has published rules and regulations in an attempt to prevent further environmental damage.

> **4** Use a table or draw a diagram to describe the advantages and disadvantages that tourism has brought to the Red Sea coast.

◀ *3.5 Diving in the Red Sea*

4 Enquiry: Masai Mara Safari, Kenya

In this Enquiry you will design a short safari in one Africa's most popular nature reserves, the Masai Mara National Reserve in Kenya. Then you can produce a brochure advertising your holiday.

Your manager has written a brief (Figure 4.1) to help you and to give you some instructions. Once you have read it, carefully work through the Enquiry Steps 1–4.

4.1 Brief for Safari trip to Masai Mara, Kenya ▼

- The Masai Mara safari will last for four nights giving three full days 'on safari'. The tourists will then fly to Mombasa on the coast for three nights to enjoy the beaches.

- Tourists should be able to see as many different animals as possible.

- Tourists will arrive by air from Nairobi.

- Transport in the reserve will be by minibus.

- The safari should only run when the weather is likely to be good.

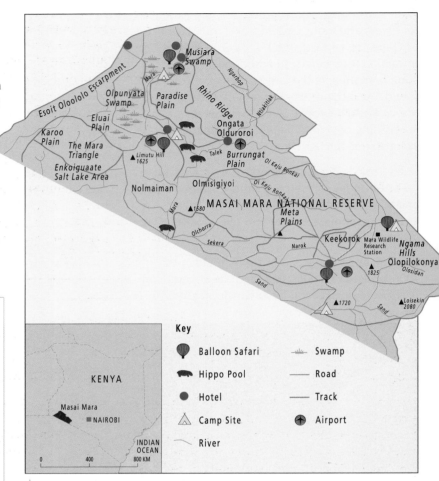

▲ 4.2 Map of the Masai Mara National Reserve

4.3 Wildebeest crossing the river in July and August is a popular tourist spectacle. ▶

▼ 4.4 Climate data for Nairobi

	J	F	M	A	M	J	J	A	S	O	N	D
Average Maximum Daily Temperature (°C)	25	26	25	24	22	21	21	21	24	24	23	23
Average Monthly Rainfall (mm)	38	64	125	211	158	46	15	23	31	53	109	86

ENQUIRY Step 1

1 Make a list of the attractions of the Reserve (Figure 4.2). Are there certain times of year when it is best to visit?

2 Take time to read through the information in this unit. Look at the map (Figure 4.2) and the photograph and try to get a feel for the Masai Mara Reserve.

3 Look at the climate information (Table 4.4) to see what the weather is likely to be at the time of year that you identified in Activity 1 above. Try to avoid very hot or very wet months.

4.5 The Masai Mara National Reserve

The Masai Mara, opened in 1974, is probably the most famous and most visited Reserve in Kenya. It offers breathtaking views of the African bush and boasts the "big five" : lions, elephants, leopards, buffalo and rhinoceros. Hippos and crocodiles inhabit the rivers.

An impressive feature is the annual migration of wildebeest, zebras and gazelles to the Mara's grasslands from across the border in Tanzania. From late June, the herds sweep across the grasslands and across the rivers tracked by their predators (lions, leopards, and cheetahs) often with vultures circling overhead. Their dramatic river crossings are a reality for tourists visiting in July-August.

(Based on Kilimanjaro Adventure Travel's website - 'www. kilimanjaro.com/')

ENQUIRY Step 2

Decide what sort of accommodation to use. Look at the information below. You will need to sell its advantages in your brochure.

Option A: Hotel

Hotels in Masai are called lodges. They provide high-quality accommodation, often in the form of single storey blocks or separate chalets. They have en-suite facilities (bath/shower, w.c.) and usually afford good views of the surrounding area. Most have verandahs from where game can be viewed at nearby watering holes.

Option B: Luxury camping

Many small camp sites offer luxury camping with an 'open air' natural feel to them. Toilets and showers are located in a separate building and a special dining tent is where meals are taken. Many camps are located close to rivers where hippos and other game can be observed in the evening, whilst sitting round an open fire.

ENQUIRY Step 3

Look carefully at Figure 4.2. Work in rough to plan the details of your trip.

1 Where do you want your safari to go? Try to offer as much variety as you can. Choose one of the locations on Figure 4.2. All four nights must be spent at the same location. Remember that the tourists will fly in to the reserve.

2 Use Figure 4.2 to suggest which routes to take for the three full-day safaris. Be careful to avoid too much travelling.

ENQUIRY Step 4

It is now time to produce your brochure advertising your safari. It is up to you what to say and how to lay out the information.
Your brochure should include the following:
- a written introduction describing the attractions of the Masai Mara reserve
- a climate graph using the data in Table 4.4
- details of the accommodation
- a map of the key locations in the reserve
- a list (called an itinerary) of what will happen during the three full days. Include location and route maps.

Cities

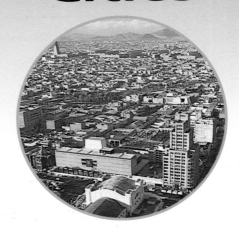

In 1998, 44% of the world's population (2.6 billion people) lived in cities. By 2025 this number is expected to double to over 5 billion people, as more and more people move to cities to live. But many of those who move to the cities in search of a better life are disappointed. A lack of jobs, poor quality housing and high levels of pollution are the features that most commonly greet the newcomers.

1 The growth of world cities

The number of people living in urban areas is increasing very rapidly and it is expected to rise even faster in the future. Look at Figure 1.1. Notice that most of this growth is taking place in the economically developing world.

In the economically developing world most people still live in the countryside and make a living by farming. In Asia only 34% of the population currently live in cities and in Africa the figure is only 31%. However, every day some 150,000 people around the world move to the cities. This is the same as a city the size of Blackpool being created each day.

In contrast, in the economically developed world, some 73% of people already live in cities. This figure is increasing only very slightly (see Figure 1.1) and it is probably close to its maximum. Indeed, some large cities such as London are beginning to see a decline, as people decide to move to smaller towns and villages in the surrounding countryside.

Why are cities growing?

The increase in the percentage of people living in towns and cities is called **urbanisation.** In the economically developing world urbanisation is very rapid for two main reasons:

1 Birth rates are high in cities. Children are needed to help earn money and to support parents in old age. There are a lot of young married couples who are able to have large families.

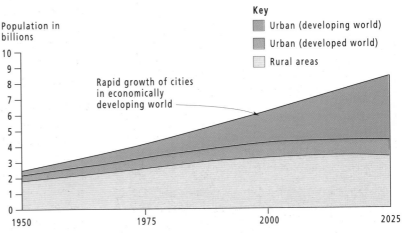

1.1 World urban population growth 1950–2025

2 Large numbers of migrants flood into the cities from the countryside.

Migration from the countryside to the city is often the result of greater levels of poverty in the countryside. In addition, people may be affected by natural disasters or poor harvests. Together these factors are called **push factors** because they encourage people to move away from the countryside (see Figure 1.2).

In comparison, cities often appear glamorous. There are bright lights, roads full of cars and lorries and the promise of better jobs and a higher standard of living. These are **pull factors** (see Figure 1.2) that act like a magnet pulling people to the cities. Unfortunately, the cities often fail to live up to the migrants expectations (see Photo 1.4).

1.2 Push and pull factors ▶

1 Study Figure 1.1.

a Use the graph to suggest how many people in 1950 lived in
- rural areas
- cities (economically developed)
- cities (economically developing)

b Repeat (a) for the year 2025.

c Write a couple of sentences describing the changes between 1950 and 2025.

d What is the meaning of the term 'urbanisation'?

e What causes cities to grow in size?

Case study: migration to Lima, Peru

▼ *1.4 Lima, Peru*

▼ *1.3 Push and pull factors in Peru*

Push factors (from the Andes)

Any grazing land is poor quality and can only be used for sheep
Most houses have no electricity or running water
Drought in the south has caused disastrous harvests of potatoes, the Indian's staple crop
Job losses in the mining industry
Much of land is too high for farming

Pull factors (to Lima)

Work on farms growing cotton, sugar cane, rice and bananas
Work in the anchovy fishing industry in harbours and factories
Electricity and piped water is available in many parts of Lima
Schools and hospitals are more widely available than in the Andes
There are many factories in Lima

Case study: migration to Lima, Peru
(continued)

Peru is twice the size of France and four times the size of the UK. Locate the country on Atlas Map B (pages 12–13). Now look at the map of Peru (page 69) to see that Peru borders the Pacific Ocean and that the Andes mountain range runs down the spine of the country.

Peru is a country of contrasts. It can be divided into three very different regions.

1 The coastal strip is very dry and, in the south, forms part of the Atacama Desert. Peru's capital city Lima (Photo 1.4) is found here. Its current population is 6.5 million people and it is growing rapidly.

▲ **1.5 Life is hard for people living in the Andes mountains**

2 The Andes mountains form a hostile landscape of high peaks and deep river valleys (see Photo 1.5). Until the 1960s it was the most densely populated part of Peru. The ancient capital of the Incas was at Cuzco. The people, most of whom are involved in farming, have adapted to living and working at these high altitudes.

3 The tropical rainforest is the lowland region to the east of the Andes. Much of this area is drained by the River Amazon. This hot and densely forested region is sparsely populated and has few major towns.

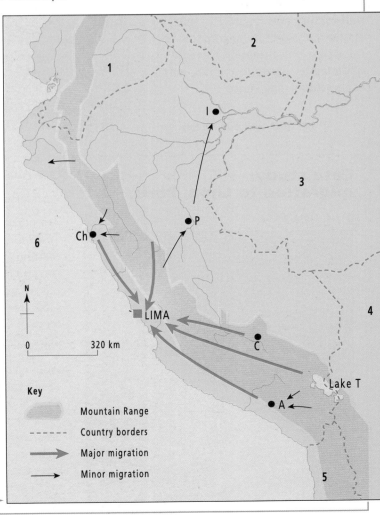

2 Study Figures 1.2 and 1.3.

a Write your own definitions of the terms 'push' and 'pull' factors.

b Construct a table identifying some examples of push and pull factors. Use Figures 1.2 and 1.3 to help you but try to add a few more yourself.

3 Study Photo 1.4. Suggest some problems that might result from large-scale migration to cities like Lima.

1.6 Migrations in Peru ▶

Key

Mountain Range
Country borders
Major migration
Minor migration

1.7 Peru ▶

4 Study Figures 1.6 and 7.

a Describe the location of Lima, Peru's capital city.

b Name the five other towns on Figure 1.6.

c What is the name of the lake in the south of the country?

d Name the five countries (1–5) that share borders with Peru.

5 Study Figure 1.6.

a From which region have most of the migrants to Lima travelled?

b Before travelling to Lima, some migrants spend time in two smaller cities. What are the names of these two cities?

c Look at Photo 1.5. Suggest some reasons (push factors) why you think people would want to leave this area.

6 Work with your neighbour or in small groups to suggest what could be done to try to encourage people to stay in the Andes mountains (see Photo 1.5) rather than move to cities such as Lima.

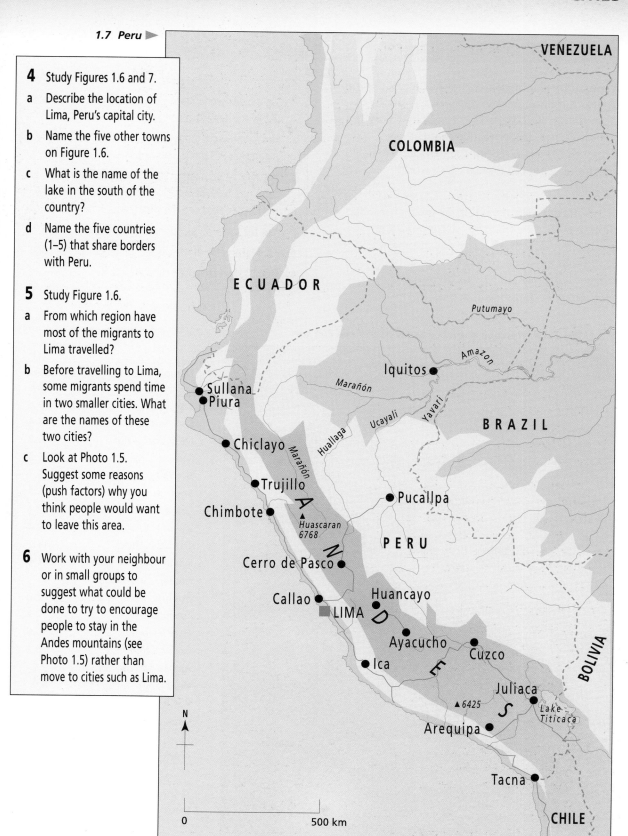

CITIES

2 Megacities

A **megacity** is a huge city that has a population of over 8 million people. Look at the photo of Paris (Photo 2.1). Paris is the only megacity in the whole of Europe. Notice that the city stretches for as far as the eye can see. This enormous extent is typical of all world megacities.

In 1995 there were a total of 22 megacities (see Table 2.2). Notice that the vast majority are located in the economically developing world. By 2015 there are expected to be a total of 33 megacities, of which 27 will be in the economically developing world.

1 On a blank world map, plot the information in Table 2.2 as a series of bars.

a Use Atlas Map B (pages 12–13) to locate each of the megacities in Table 2.2 on to a blank world outline.

b Present the population values for each city in the form of a bar. Work out a vertical scale. Try 1 cm = 5 million people. Keep the width of each bar the same.

c Use the same colour to shade all of the bars.

d Write the name of the city alongside each of the bars.

e Don't forget to write your scale in a key.

▼ **2.1 The Paris cityscape stretches as far as the eye can see**

2.2 The world's megacities (1995)

Megacity	Population (millions)
Tokyo, Japan	26.8
Sao Paulo, Brazil	16.4
New York, USA	16.3
Mexico City, Mexico	15.6
Bombay, India	15.1
Shanghai, China	15.1
Los Angeles, USA	12.4
Beijing, China	12.4
Calcutta, India	11.7
Seoul, Rep. of Korea	11.6
Jakarta, Indonesia	11.
Buenos Aires, Argentina	11.0
Tianjin, China	10.7
Osaka, Japan	10.6
Lagos, Nigeria	10.3
Rio de Janeiro, Brazil	9.9
New Delhi, India	9.9
Karachi, Pakistan	9.9
Cairo, Egypt	9.7
Paris, France	9.5
Manila, Philippines	9.3
Moscow, Russian Fed.	9.2

(Source: World Resources Institute 1996–7)

70

Living in megacities

Megacities throughout the world show great contrasts between the rich and the poor. All megacities have some areas of great wealth, with classy shopping centres and posh apartment blocks (Photo 2.3). However, they also have areas of great poverty (Photo 2.4).

▲ *2.3 High income area*

◄ *2.4 Low income area*

Most cities in the economically developing world have large areas of houses. These are called **shanties**. Constructed from scraps of timber and metal, these houses are usually built by new migrants to the city, often on land that they do not own. Without running water, electricity or proper sanitation, conditions are very poor and disease is rife.

Megacities are living and working cities. They contain large industrial areas often alongside rivers or sea ports. Many companies have their headquarters in megacities and there are important administrative functions such as government buildings, stock exchanges and major financial institutions. In addition, there are areas for recreation, such as public parks, theatres, cinemas, galleries and sports stadiums.

---

2 Study Photo 2.4.

a What name is given to low income housing in cities in the economically developing world?

b Describe the characteristics of the houses shown in Photo 2.4.

c What are living conditions likely to be like in the area of the photo?

d Why do you think the people have had to build these houses?

e What do you think the local authority could do to improve the shanty housing shown in Photo 2.4?

3 City street children

Ramu is twelve years old. He lives in Bombay, India with his six-year-old sister and three-year-old brother. The children were thrown out of their house by their step-father. Find out more about Ramu and his life on the streets of Bombay by reading his story in Figure 3.1.

1 Read through Ramu's story in Figure 3.1 and attempt the following questions.

a How do Ramu and his friends find food to eat?

b Where do they hide and find shelter in Bombay?

c What are Ramu's dreams for the future?

d Do you think he will achieve his ambitions? Explain your answer.

2 Study Figure 3.2.

a Which country has the greatest number of street children?

b Which European country has the greatest number of recorded street children?

c Do you think that the issue of street children affects the whole world or just some parts only?

▼ 3.1 Ramu

Ramu leads a small group of street children who steal fruit and small items to sell. The group also survive by eating banana peel and fruit pulp thrown out by restaurants. The narrow alleys, railway sidings and deserted construction sites are the hiding places for his street-family. Ramu wants to own a market stall and a hotel when he is older. That way he will have money and a place for his small group. He says he has no time for school now because he is far too busy looking after the others.

▼ 3.2 Street children around the world

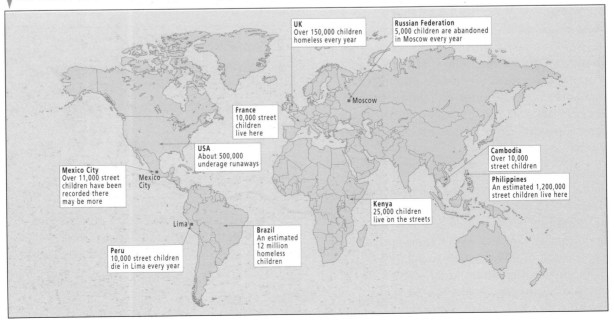

UK
Over 150,000 children homeless every year

Russian Federation
5,000 children are abandoned in Moscow every year

Moscow

France
10,000 street children live here

USA
About 500,000 underage runaways

Cambodia
Over 10,000 street children

Mexico City
Over 11,000 street children have been recorded there may be more

Mexico City

Philippines
An estimated 1,200,000 street children live here

Kenya
25,000 children live on the streets

Lima

Brazil
An estimated 12 million homeless children

Peru
10,000 street children die in Lima every year

Surviving on the street

Life on the city streets is very dangerous. Street children may be rounded-up by the police, beaten and even killed. In order to survive many form gangs so that they can look out for each other.

Children find many ways to earn some money. They act as porters at bus or railway stations, mind cars for people at work or shopping, or they scavenge rags and other waste products from rubbish tips to sell. A good many turn to prostitution and others have no choice but to beg for money.

The poor diet and lack of shelter leads to many health problems amongst the children, such as skin diseases and pneumonia. In addition, drug abuse and prostitution is leading to an increase in the spread of AIDS.

Helping the world's street children

Several charities work to improve the life of street children by providing shelter, food and security.

Jubilee Action is one such charity. It funds Girls' Homes in India and Brazil. The Princess Diana Home for Girls in Rio de Janeiro, Brazil takes care of some twenty girls and their children (see Photo 3.3). The girls are well cared for, safe, happy and they have a future to look forward to.

Jubilee Action is helping boys in Uganda's capital city Kampala through the support of a football club (Figure 3.4). Over 100 boys have formed the Tiger Club and their football team has taken part in, and won, a number of youth competitions. Jubilee Action is supporting the boys by funding a medical centre and an education centre. Money is also being used to help provide shelter and food for some of Kampala's 2,000 street children.

> **3** Write a few sentences decribing life on the streets for street children. How do they survive and what problems do they face?

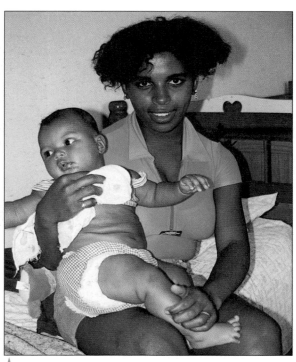

3.3 Teenage mother and child at the Princess Diana Home for Girls in Rio de Janiero

3.4 The Tiger Club, Kampala, Uganda ▶

4 ENQUIRY: issues in Mexico City

You may wish to use the information in this Enquiry to produce a longer project on Mexico City or, alternatively, you can work through the activities at the end of each Enquiry Box. The Internet is a good source of information on Mexico City.

ENQUIRY A

Mexico City: an introduction

Mexico City is the capital of Mexico (Figure A1). It is one of the largest and most rapidly growing cities in the world, with a population in excess of 25 million people in the city and suburbs. Mexico City is so huge that, from the top of its highest skyscraper, it stretches for as far as the eye can see (Photo A2).

A1 Mexico

A2 An aerial view of Mexico City

In common with cities the world over, Mexico City is a city of great contrasts (Photo A3). It is noisy, dirty, and smelly, yet it is also vibrant, exciting and, in places, very beautiful. The centre of Mexico City (Photo A4) is a bustling and colourful place. The roads heave with yellow taxi-cabs and old buses, and the streets are lined with traders selling fast food, drinks and crafts. Everywhere is the sound of car hooters, police whistles and the constant chatter of the city people going about their business.

1 Draw a sketch map of Mexico to show the location of Mexico City. Use Atlas Maps A and B (pages 10–11 and 12–13) to help you locate and label the following features on to your map:
- Sierra Madre mountain range
- Yucatan
- Pacific Ocean
- Tropic of Cancer
- Belize
- Gulf of Mexico
- Rio Grande
- USA
- Guatemala

2 Use the photos to help you write a few sentences describing some of the characteristics of Mexico City.

3 Why do you think Mexico City is attractive to tourists?

A3 The streets of Mexico City are colourful and vibrant

A4 Mexico City is bustling with people and cars

ENQUIRY B Pollution

Most of the time, a view from the rooftops is like Photo B1. The misty haze that you can see is caused by pollution – it is called **smog**. Smog is a thick, dirty form of fog that contains particles of dust and other pollutants.

Dust and fumes from Mexico City's many industries, together with exhaust emissions from 3 million vehicles, fills the air with a dirty, metallic-tasting cocktail of gases. Just breathing the air is said to be as harmful as smoking 40 cigarettes a day. It is only a matter of hours before new arrivals to the city complain of sore throats. Look at Figure B2 to discover why the location of Mexico City makes the problem worse.

The city authorities are attempting to reduce levels of pollution by the following measures:

- private cars have to be kept off the road for one day a week. Different coloured number plates are used to monitor the system.

- during periods of serious pollution, industries are shut down

- buses and lorries are being converted to run on less-polluting fuels such as natural gas

▲ *B1 View over Mexico city during smog*

1 What is smog and how is it caused?

2 Make a sketch of the diagram below to show how the location of Mexico City makes the problem of pollution worse.

3 What is being done to reduce levels of pollution? Can you suggest other measures that could be introduced?

B2 Mexico City's physical geography makes the pollution problem worse ▼

Heavy cold air sinks into the Valley of Mexico

Smoke and fumes trapped by the cold air

Winter

MEXICO CITY

Water supply

ENQUIRY C

Imagine what it must be like for a city authority trying to supply safe water to the millions of people that live in Mexico City.

An estimated 60,000 litres of water is consumed every second in Mexico City. The vast majority of the water is pumped up from groundwater sources 70-300 metres below Mexico City.

The huge and ever increasing demand for water is already causing a number of serious problems

● demand is exceeding supply, causing the level of the underground water to drop. As water levels drop, wells dry up and have to be sunk deeper into the rocks.

● as water levels have fallen, the overlying sands and clays have sunk. This has led to subsidence on the surface, causing buildings to sink several metres below street level.

● the main sewage pipeline (built in 1900) has sunk too so that gravity no longer carries the waste away from Mexico City (Figure C1). Pumps now have to be used along the old pipeline and a brand new deeper pipeline (the Profundo) has had to be constructed.

For the future, water may have to be piped from rivers that are over 100 km from the city. In the meantime, people are being encouraged to conserve water and the local authorities are working to repair the broken pipes that result in a massive loss of water.

---

1 Read the section on water supply.

a Where does Mexico City get most of its water from?

b Why are water levels falling?

2 Make a copy of Figure C1.

a How many water wells supply Mexico City?

b How many wells are below a depth of 100 metres?

c What is the name of the original sewage pipeline?

d Why have pumping stations been built along the route of the pipeline?

e Why does sewage flow more easily along the new Profundo pipeline?

3 Suggest ways in which people might conserve water. Design a poster or newspaper advert to encourage people to use less water. Illustrate your work with simple sketches or diagrams.

▼ *C1 Water supply and sewage disposal in Mexico City*

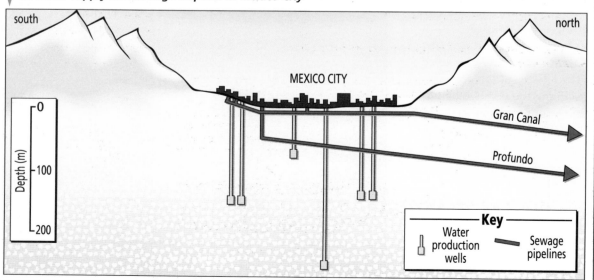

Environmental and Resource Issues

People are increasingly concerned about the quality of our environment. During the last century, human activity caused a great deal of environmental damage to the land, the seas and the air. We are part of the natural world and need to learn to live with it in a sustainable way.

1 Global environmental and resource issues

In 1998 an alarming report was published by the Worldwide Fund for Nature. It suggested that, in the last 25 years, plants and animals had suffered a drop of more than 30% in their numbers in forests, freshwaters and the seas. The main reason for this decline was thought to be human activity, for example, cutting down areas of rainforest. The report was one of several that were published in the late twentieth century describing the damage being done to our environment.

1.1 Rainforests are often cleared using the process of 'slash and burn'. The rainforest in north eastern Madagascar has been completely cleared ▶

▲ **1.2 In this toxic waste dump, fuel drums have been left to rust away**

Look at Atlas Map C (pages 80–81) and study the key to discover the range of environmental threats currently facing the world. Some of these threats are illustrated by the photos 1.1 and 12. Notice that not all the threats are to the 'natural' world. Air pollution, for example, is a serious problem in many of the world's major cities.

Why is the environment under threat?

Much of the environmental damage identified on Atlas Map C (pages 80–81) and that which we read about in newspapers, or see on the television, results from human activity. As we strive to become better off, so the environment often suffers. Industry uses up valuable resources and pollutes the air with its gases. Forests are cut down to make way for intensive farming or settlement, as demands from a growing population increase. The seas become polluted by waste and by the transport of oil that is used to fire our industries and power our cars.

A sustainable future?

Nowadays there is an increasing belief that people need to live in harmony with nature so that future generations do not suffer from our actions. You have already come across this belief in Books 1 and 2. It is called **sustainability**.

1 Study Photos 1.1) and 1.2). For each photo, describe what it shows and suggest why it is a threat to the environment.

2 Study Atlas Map C on pages 80–81. You might also find it helpful to refer to Atlas Maps A and B (pages 10–11 and 12–13).

a What threats to the environment are located close to the UK?

b Name two areas of the world where rainforests are under threat.

c What do you notice about the location of many of the nuclear test sites? What does this suggest to you about the dangers of such tests?

d Look at the key and find how 'river pollution' is shown. Name the major river system in each of the following countries that has been identified as being polluted:
- USA
- Argentina
- Iraq (there are two rivers here)
- Australia
- Egypt

e Choose a region of the world that you are interested in, for example, South America, Australia or Africa. For your chosen region, draw a map (using a blank outline if you have one) to show the environmental threats. Use colours and symbols, and don't forget to explain them in a key. Write a few sentences describing the threats to your chosen region.

3 Read the section on sustainability.

a Describe in your own words the meaning of 'sustainability'.

b How can forests be managed in a sustainable way? Use a series of simple diagrams to illustrate your answer.

c Do you think the idea of living in a sustainable way is a good idea? Explain your answer.

Living sustainably means being less wasteful by conserving resources like energy and water, rather than simply seeking to find more. It involves planting trees as well as chopping them down, so that there will always be a steady supply in the future. It also involves reducing pollution which is known to harm the environment as well as ourselves.

THREATS TO THE ENVIRONMENT

- Tropical rain forest
- Severe marine pollution
- River pollution
- Current nuclear test site
- Former nuclear test site
- Major city with air pollution problem due to industry and vehicle exhaust
- Offshore oil production

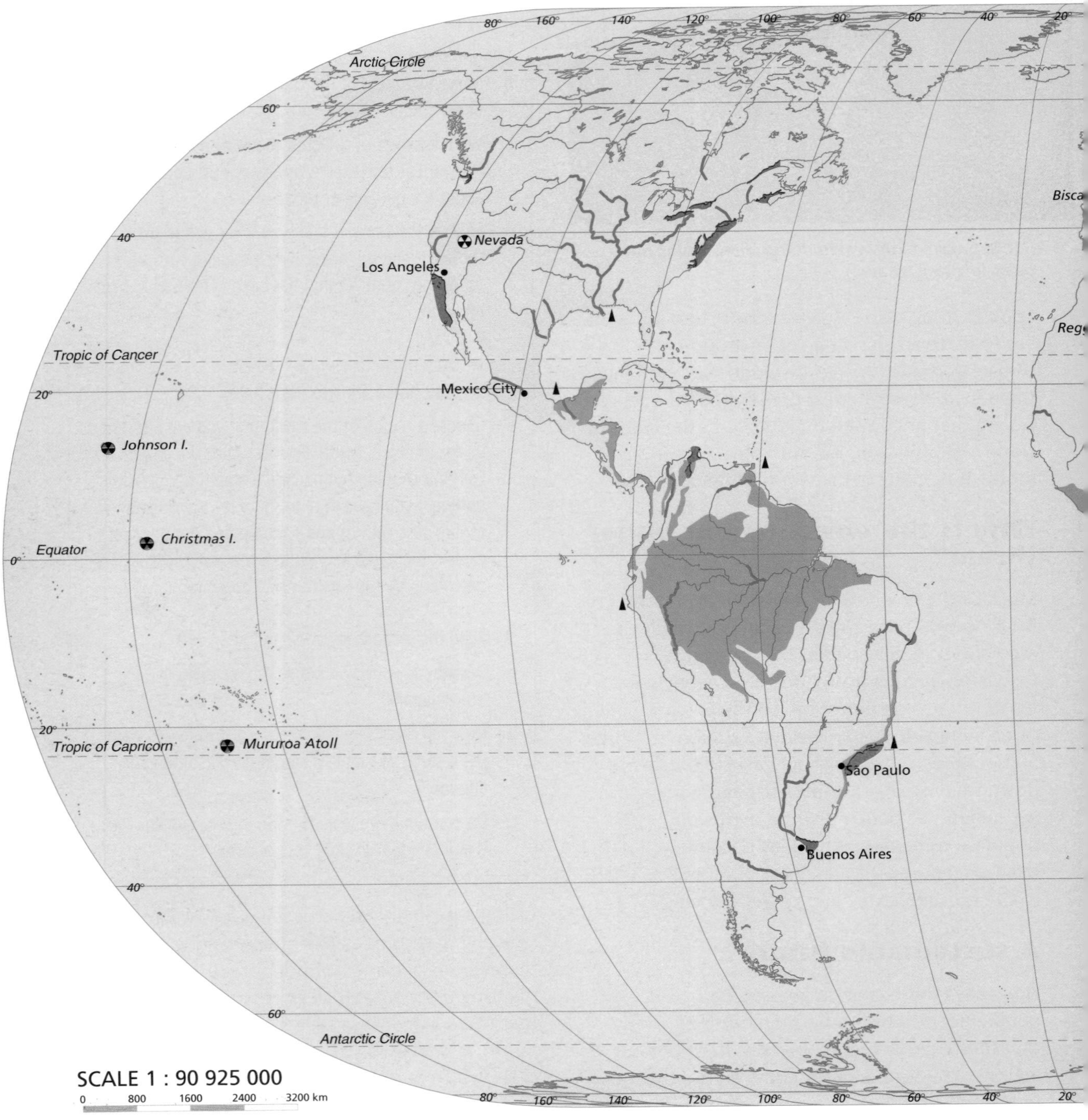

Arctic Circle
60°
40°
Tropic of Cancer
20°
Equator
0°
20°
Tropic of Capricorn
40°
60°
Antarctic Circle
80°
160°
140°
120°
100°
80°
60°
40°
20°
Nevada
Los Angeles
Mexico City
Johnson I.
Christmas I.
Mururoa Atoll
São Paulo
Buenos Aires
Bisca
Reg

SCALE 1 : 90 925 000

0 800 1600 2400 3200 km

ATLAS MAP C
The global environment

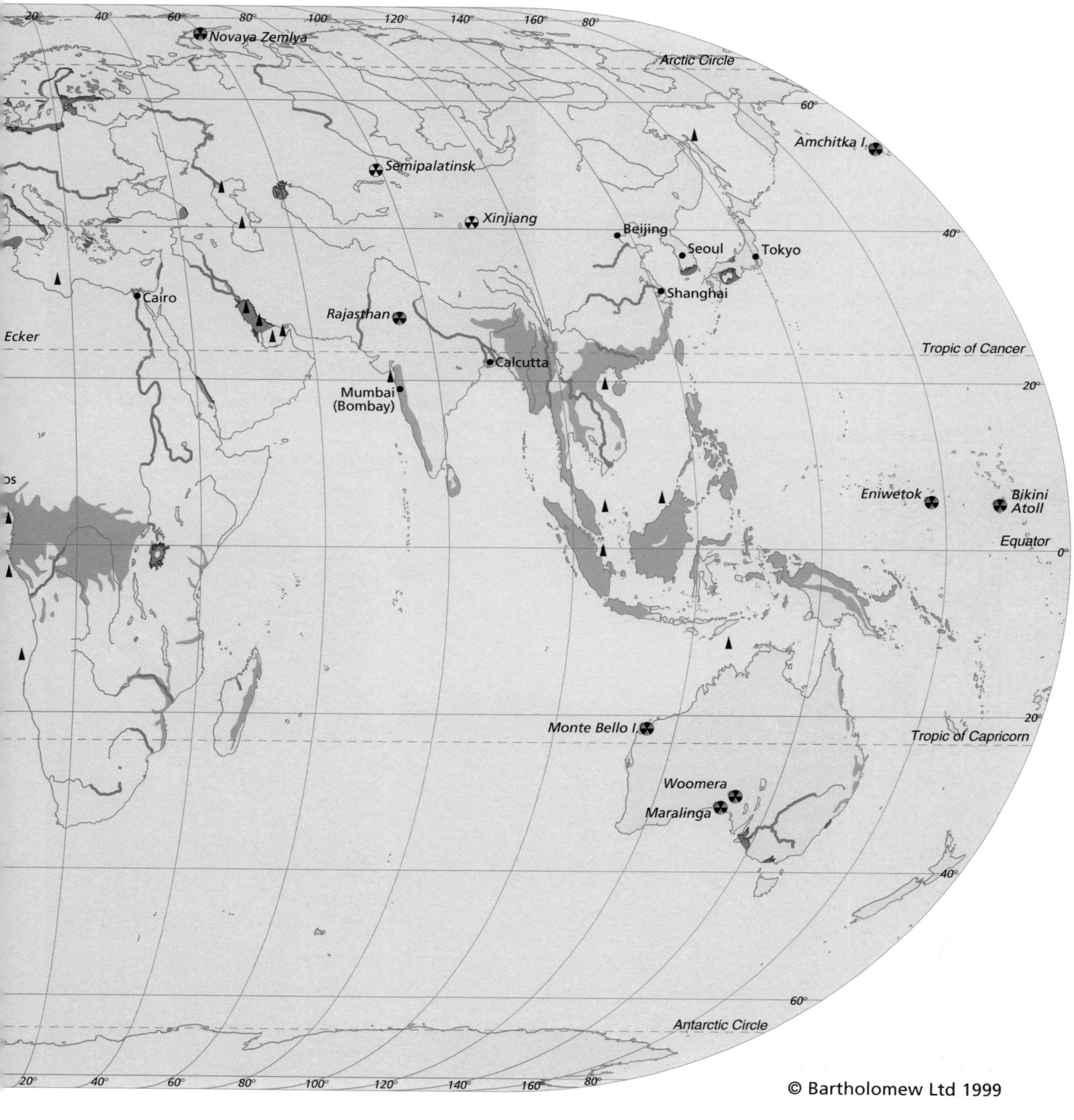

Novaya Zemlya

Arctic Circle

60°

Amchitka I.

Semipalatinsk

Xinjiang

Beijing

40°

Seoul   Tokyo

Cairo

Shanghai

Ecker

Rajasthan

Tropic of Cancer

20°

Calcutta

Mumbai
(Bombay)

os

Eniwetok

Bikini
Atoll

Equator

0°

20°

Monte Bello I.

Tropic of Capricorn

Woomera

Maralinga

40°

60°

Antarctic Circle

© Bartholomew Ltd 1999

2 Tropical rainforests

Walking into a rainforest is a truly amazing experience. There are tall trees stretching into the sky and huge plants of all shapes and sizes, mostly with sheet-like dark green leaves (Photo 2.1). Inside the rainforest much of the light from the sun is shaded by the trees' leaves and branches. It is very hot and steamy and the heavy rainfall makes the forest floor damp and spongy to walk on. It is also incredibly noisy with a confusion of sound from insects, birds and howler monkeys .

One characteristic typical of rainforests is that the vegetation forms a number of distinct layers. Look at Figure 2.2 and notice that three layers can be identified. The upper layer's leaves and branches form an almost continuous umbrella called a **canopy**. In places individual trees can break through the canopy to grow over 50 metres high!

2.1 This rainforest in Grenada has been turned into a National Park

▼ 2.2 The vertical structure of a rainforest

2.3 The Dayak people collect rattan which is used in furniture-making

What is special about rainforests

Biodiversity: Rainforests have more species (types) of plant and animal than any other environment on earth. Some species are becoming extinct because rainforests are being cut down.

Science: Chemicals found in rainforest plants have been used to treat bronchitis, epilepsy and leukemia. There are almost certainly others which have yet to be discovered.

People: Throughout the world, rainforests are home to 200 million tribal people who live in harmony with nature.

The advance of western civilisation, however has caused widespread disease. In Brazil one Amazonian tribe has been lost for every year of the 20th century.

Climate: Rainforests are thought to have an effect on our climate. Trees return water to the atmosphere and use up carbon dioxide. Without the trees, our climate could become much drier and might accelerate global warming.

1 Study Figure 2.2.

a Use the scale on the left-hand axis of the diagram to find the approximate heights of the three layers of vegetation.

b What is meant by the tree canopy?

c Suggest what might happen to the soil if the trees were cut down.

2 Study the information and photos about rainforests.

a How important are rainforests as homes for species of plants and animals?

b In what ways do local people make use of the resources of the forests? (Look at Photo 2.3.)

c How has science benefited from the plants that live in rainforests?

d In what ways do tropical rainforests influence our climate?

▼ *2.4 The location of rainforests*

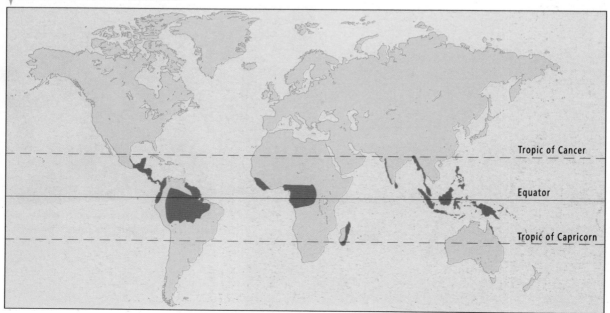

Tropic of Cancer

Equator

Tropic of Capricorn

Where are tropical rainforests found?

Tropical rainforests are found in a discontinuous belt stretching through the tropics from Central and South America in the west, to Indonesia and Australia in the east (see Figure 2.4). In the past they covered a much greater area than today.

Temperatures remain at about 25°C throughout the year and the annual average rainfall exceeds 1,500 mm. Rainfall often occurs as torrential thunderstorms, usually in the early afternoon.

Rainforests under threat

Scientists believe that 50% of the world's rainforests have been cleared in the last 200 years, with the bulk of this being in the last 50 years. The removal of trees is called **deforestation** and it has had dramatic effects on the plants and animals that live in the rainforests. Already many rainforest species have become extinct and others will surely follow if the destruction is not halted.

> **3** For this activity you will need a blank world outline. Study the map of rainforests in Figure 2.4.
>
> **a** Use a pencil to draw the areas of tropical rainforest on to your map. Then use a colour to shade the areas and make them stand out more clearly.
>
> **b** Draw and label (using Atlas Map A pages 10–11) the following lines of latitude:
> - the Equator
> - the Tropic of Cancer
> - the Tropic of Capricorn
>
> **c** Now use Atlas Maps A and B (pages 10–11 and 12–13) to complete your map by labelling the regions and countries where tropical rainforests are located.
>
> **d** Write a sentence describing the global distribution of tropical rainforests.

▼ **2.6 Aerial view of opencast mines in the Amazon**

▲ **2.5 Rainforests are cleared to make way for cattle ranches like this one in Bolivia**

Tropical rainforests are being chopped down for several reasons:

1 Timber. Most trees in the rainforest are known as hardwoods. They include trees such as mahogany and teak which are highly valued for their use in furniture-making.

2 Farmland. In some parts of the world rainforests have been cleared to make way for extensive cattle ranching or for the creation of plantations to grow commercial crops like palm oil or rubber.

3 Raw materials. In the Amazon region of Brazil, there are rich mineral reserves such as copper and iron in the rainforest. Huge opencast mines have caused enormous destruction to the rainforest (see Photo 2.6)

Managing rainforests in Malaysia

In the past, almost all of Malaysia (Figure 2.8) was clothed by tropical rainforest. Today only about 59% remains and much of this is replanted commercial forest as opposed to virgin (untouched) rainforest.

Vast areas of forest have been cut down over the years to make way for agriculture, particularly commercial plantations where oil palms and rubber trees have been grown. These products have been exported to help pay for Malaysia's recent industrialisation.

4 Study Table 2.7.

a Plot flowlines on to a blank world map outline to show the export of mahogany from the Brazilian port of Belem (situated at the mouth of the River Amazon).
- Work out a scale so that the thickness of each flowline is proportional to the amount of tonnes exported. Draw the lines on your map and colour them.
- Label Brazil, Belem and each country that imports mahogany.

2.7 Trade in Brazilian mahogany from the port of Belem, Brazil, 1992 ▼

Destination	cubic metres of mahogany
Venezuela	1 370
Japan	40
Caribbean	6 600
USA	46 580
UK	31 323
Rest of Europe	18 768
Total	104 681

(Source: FOE)

b Which two countries import the greatest amount of mahogany? Are the two countries MEDCs or LEDCs?

c Much of the world's tropical rainforests are found in LEDCs. Suggest why these countries often feel the need to exploit their rainforests.

Carry out some additional research by using library books, CD-ROMs (such as Encarta) and by conducting searches on the Internet.

▼ *2.8 Malaysia*

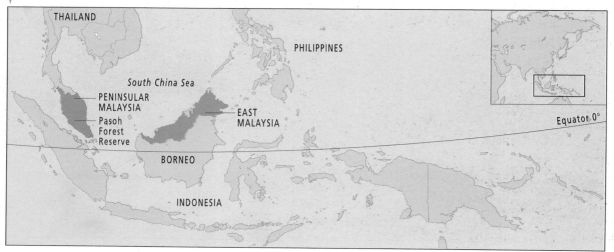

The government soon realised, however, that it was unsustainable for the future. In the early 1970s a detailed study of Malaysia's land use was carried out. It was decided that these Permanent Forest Estates areas could not be used for any purpose other than forestry.

In 1977 the National Forestry Act introduced a new way of managing forests. It is called the Selective Management System (SMS) (Figure 2.9). The SMS is recognised as being one of the most successful sustainable forms of forestry management in the world. Study Figure 2.9 to discover how it works.

2.8 Rubber plantation in Malaysia

5 Study Figure 2.9.

a Why do you think it is important to carry out a pre-felling survey?

b Why is it important to decide the direction of felling for each tree?

c Only larger trees are felled. Why do you think this is?

d Do you think it is important that only licenced fellers can cut down trees? Why?

2.9 Sustainable forestry: the Selective Management System ▼

2 years before felling
survey to identify what is there

1 year before felling
trees that are fully grown are marked for felling. Direction of felling to be marked on trees

30–40 years before felling
cycle starts again

Felling
carried out by licence holders only

5–10 years after felling
new trees planted in places where old trees were felled

2 years after felling
survey to identify where new trees should be planted

6 months after felling
survey to check which trees were felled. People can be prosecuted if illegal felling has occurred.

(Source: Tropical Forests FSC)

3 Coral reefs: the rainforests of the sea

Coral reefs (Photo 3.1) are one of the most colourful and spectacular natural environments on Earth. They are the ocean's richest ecosystem (see Figure 3.2) which is why some people have described them as the 'rainforests of the sea'. If you have been lucky enough to go snorkelling or diving over a coral reef you will probably have seen a great variety of fish, plants and animals.

A coral reef is a living and growing landform. Each reef is made of the hard outer skeletons (called exoskeletons) of millions of tiny living corals. The corals feed on the algae (tiny plants) that grow on the reef. Corals are extremely sensitive to environmental change, for example changes in water temperature, clarity or chemistry. Recently people have been very concerned to discover that large areas of the world's coral reefs are dying.

1 Study Photo 3.1.

a Make a list of adjectives (describing words) describing the photo.

b What is a coral reef?

c Why do you think coral reefs are sometimes described as the 'rainforests of the sea'? Do you think it is a good description?

▼ *3.1 Coral reefs are an underwater paradise*

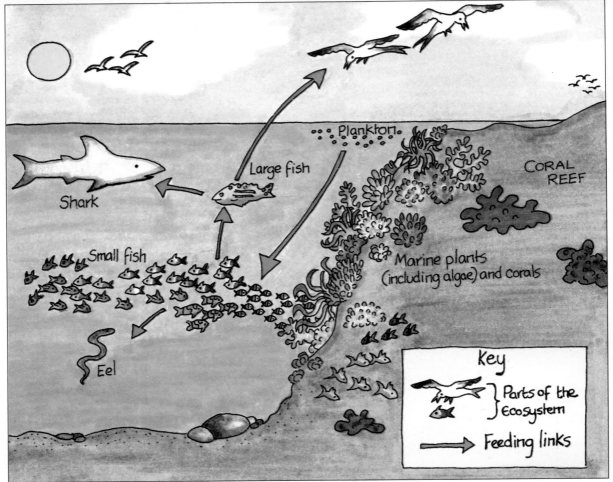

▲ 3.2 The coral reef ecosystem

Why are coral reefs important?

Coral reefs are important for several reasons:

- **Biodiversity**. Coral reefs are home to 93,000 different species of fish, plants, animals and micro-organisms.

- **Food.** About 10% of the world's annual fish catch comes from coral reefs, especially in developing regions such as Asia. It is thought that fish from coral reefs feeds over 1 billion people.

- **Tourism.** Over 100 countries, many of them poor, benefit from tourists visiting coral reefs to go snorkelling or diving.

- **Medicine.** Corals are already being used for bone grafts. Some of the chemicals produced by corals are being used to treat viruses and may be used in the future in the treatment of cancer.

- **Coastal protection.** Coral reefs act as a buffer to storms, causing waves to break early and thereby reducing damage to coastlines, and mangrove forests.

2 Study Figure 3.2.

a What is an ecosystem?

b What feeds on the plants that live on the coral reef?

c The eels and large fish are secondary consumers. Name the two tertiary consumers shown in Figure 3.2.

d What would happen to the ecosystem if the corals were destroyed?

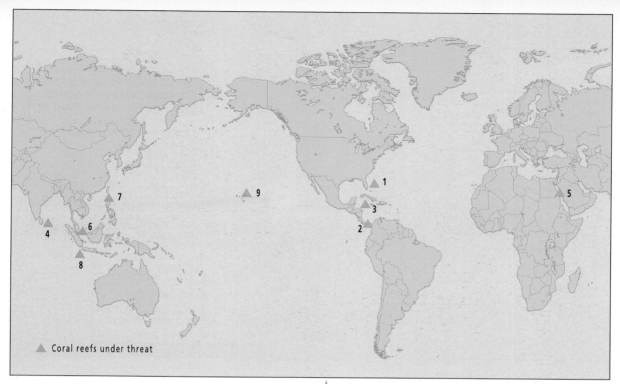

3.3 *The location of coral reefs under threat*

Corals under threat

In common with many other natural systems, coral reefs are under threat (see Figure 3.3 and Table 3.4). Large swathes of coral are dying and in some places, for example the Indian Ocean and the western Pacific around Indonesia and the Philippines, 90% of the coral is already dead.

3.4 *Threats to coral reef ecosystems around the world* ▼

Location	Threat
1 Florida Keys, USA	sewage pollution from Florida; boating; diving
2 Panama	major oil spill in 1986
3 Jamaica	sewage pollution; tourism; hurricane damage
4 Sri Lanka	tourism; coral mining; over-fishing
5 Red Sea	tourism (especially diving)
6 Singapore	sediment pollution due to dredging of shipping lanes
7 Philippines	over-fishing and the use of cyanide
8 Indonesia	sewage pollution; over-fishing; diving
9 Hawaii	increased soil erosion leading to more sediment in the water; sewage pollution; diving

---

3 Construct a colourful and informative diagram to describe the different reasons why coral reefs are important ecosystems.

a Make a large drawing showing just the outline of the coral reef in Figure 3.2. Draw this in the centre of a piece of paper.

b Now add labels around your drawing, using simple sketches or symbols, to show the reasons why coral reefs are important. Be inventive and make your diagram look attractive.

c Do you think it is important to conserve coral reefs? Explain your answer.

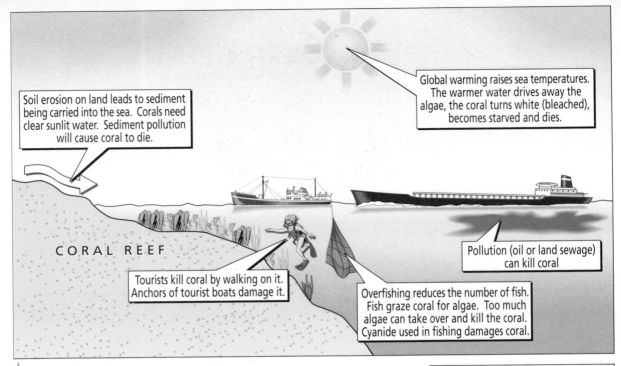

Soil erosion on land leads to sediment being carried into the sea. Corals need clear sunlit water. Sediment pollution will cause coral to die.

Global warming raises sea temperatures. The warmer water drives away the algae, the coral turns white (bleached), becomes starved and dies.

CORAL REEF

Tourists kill coral by walking on it. Anchors of tourist boats damage it.

Overfishing reduces the number of fish. Fish graze coral for algae. Too much algae can take over and kill the coral. Cyanide used in fishing damages coral.

Pollution (oil or land sewage) can kill coral

3.5 Causes of damage to coral reefs

There are several causes of damage to coral reefs as Figure 3.5 illustrates.

Scientists believe a combination of factors is responsible for the alarming damage being done to the world's coral reefs.

1 Global warming is leading to an increase in sea surface temperatures of up to 2.4°C. The result of the extra warmth is that the corals are being bleached. Bleaching happens when the higher temperatures drive away the microscopic algae that provide food for the corals. The result is that the corals turn white and, without a source of food, they starve and eventually die.

2 Pollution of the sea by oil spills or the discharge of sewage can kill coral or make it vulnerable to damage from other causes.

3 Corals need clear, sunlit waters to survive. If the waters become muddied the corals will die. In some parts of the world, soil erosion on land is leading to more sediment being dumped by rivers in reef environments

4 Tourists kill coral simply by walking on it. Anchors from tourist boats may also cause considerable damage to reefs.

5 Overfishing of reef waters can also lead to harmful effects. Fish browse the coral for algae. Without this grazing, the algae would soon take over the reef, eventually causing the coral to die. Some forms of fishing involve the use of chemicals such as cyanide which also kills coral.

4 Study Figure 3.3.

a Plot the locations of the reefs under threat on a blank map of the world.

b Now study Table 3.4. Make up some colour symbols to show the different threats.

c Draw the correct symbols alongside each threatened reef and explain the symbols in a key.

d Use Atlas Map A (pages 10–11) to label the following :-
- Pacific Ocean
- Atlantic Ocean
- Indian Ocean
- Caribbean
- Africa
- Red Sea
- India
- Australia
- Africa
- USA
- South America

Bangladesh

Bangladesh is one of the poorest and most densely populated countries in the world. Most of its people live and work in the countryside. It is often in the news because of the effects of flooding and tropical cyclones.

1 Where is Bangladesh?

Bangladesh is located in south-east Asia. Look at Figure 1.1 and notice that Bangladesh is almost completely surrounded by India. The country of Bangladesh, meaning 'land of the Bangla-speaking people' used to be part of Pakistan until it gained its independence in 1971.

Most of Bangladesh is a **delta**, a vast flat area of silt and sand deposited by rivers as they join the sea. Look at Figure 1.1 to discover the names of the three massive rivers which come together in Bangladesh before flowing into the Bay of Bengal. Whilst much of the delta is fertile land and good for farming, it is very flat and low-lying. This helps to explain why Bangladesh suffers so often from flooding.

Bangladesh has an area of 144,000 km² which makes it almost exactly the same size as England. Its population, however, is 123 million compared to England's 48 million! This gives you an idea of just how densely populated Bangladesh is.

Look at Figure 1.2 to discover more about Bangladesh.

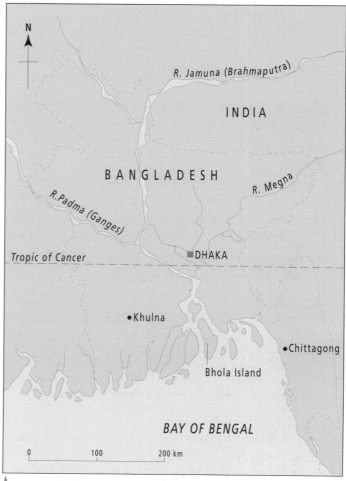

▲ *1.1 Bangladesh*

1.2 Factfile: Bangladesh

1.2a) A typical Bangladesh scene is of a low-lying area of farmland, with fields bordered by lines of trees

Today

partly cloudy
20–25°C

Saturday

partly cloudy
24–27°C

Sunday

thunderstorms
23–26°C

Monday

mostly cloudy
22–25°C

Tuesday

showers
21–25°C

1.2b) 5-day weather forecast for Dhaka, November

Bangladesh has a tropical monsoon climate, with a hot and rainy summer (June–October), a dry, cooler winter (November–February) and a hot and mostly dry spring (March–May). Even in the winter, the coolest month of January has an average temperature of 26°C.

Most of Bangladesh is used for farming (Table 1.2c). This is because the soil is fertile and the climate is favourable for growing crops such as rice, jute (used in industry for its fibres) and wheat. At the coast, fishing (especially for shrimps) has become important.

About 16% of Bangladesh is forest. A tidal forest called the Sundarbans (a swamp region in the Ganges delta) is home to the Royal Bengal tiger.

Most Bangladeshis are Bengali. They speak Bengla, which is the 6th most commonly spoken language in the world. Most people are Muslims (87%) and the rest are Hindus (12%), Christians and Buddists.

The local currency is called the Taka. One taka is worth about 2p. Many people in Bangladesh have to survive on less than 25 taka a day.

Dhaka is the capital city of Bangladesh. It is home to nearly 9 million people, considerably more than the population of London.

Arable land	67%
Permanent crops (e.g. fruit)	2%
Pasture/meadows	4%
Forest	16%
Other	11%

1.2c) Land use in Bangladesh ▶ (Source: Virtual Bangladesh, Internet)

One of the most common forms of transport is the **rickshaw**. It provides many people with a source of income and is cheap for passengers.

About 14% of the working population work in industry and mining. Most work in factories producing cotton clothes for export, or making sacking and carpet backing from the jute. Bangladesh has few mineral resources of its own.

WEB SEARCH
An excellent site with lots of information about Bangladesh exists at
//www.virtualbangladesh.com/

1.2d) Rickshaws are the main form of transport in Dhaka

1 Read the text about Bangladesh.

a What does the name 'Bangladesh' mean?

b To which country did Bangladesh belong before it became independent?

c What is a delta and how does it form?

d How much greater is Bangladesh's population than England's?

2 Study the information in Figure 1.2 and answer the following questions.

a Describe the typical Bangladesh scene as illustrated by Photo 1.2a).

b Look at Figure 1.2b).
● Describe the weather for Dhaka during the five days in November.
● What season is it in November?

c Use the information in Table 1.2c) to produce a pie chart to show land use in Bangladesh.
● Why is so much of the country used for farming?
● Suggest some possible 'other' land uses.

d What are Bangladesh's two main cereal food crops?

e What is jute and what is it used for?

f What type of fish has become an important source of income in recent years?

Satellite photograph and map study

Photo 1.3 is a satellite image of southern Bangladesh. Look carefully at the key to discover the meaning of the different colours shown on the image.

Now look at the map of Bangladesh (Atlas Map D) and try to spot some of the features on the satellite image. The rivers and coast are good starting points. Use both the map and the photograph to help you attempt the following activities.

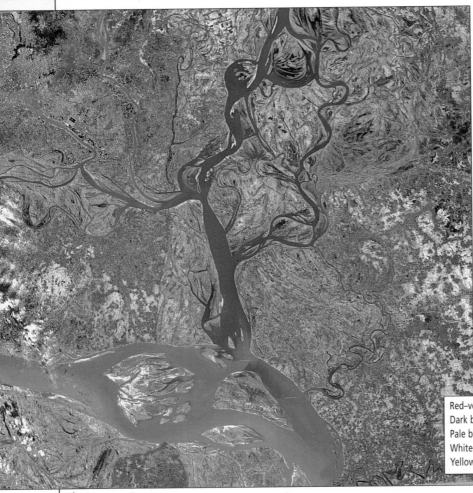

Red–vegetation
Dark blue–river water
Pale blue–river water full of silt
White– (in rivers) exposed to silt
Yellow/cream–bare soil and sparse vegetation

▲ *1.3 Satellite image of Bangladesh*

Study Atlas Map D opposite, and the satellite image, Photo 1.3. The area of the photo is shown on the map by a black square.

3

a Use the relief key on Atlas Map D to suggest the height range for much of Bangladesh.

b Describe the location of the only range of hills in the country.

c Suggest two reasons for the location of the Karnafuli Reservoir near Chittagong.

d What are the names of the two main rivers shown in Photo 1.3?

e What is the name of the urban area shown as black in the top left of Photo 1.3?

4 Look closely at the rivers in the satellite image. Notice that the channels split and rejoin in several places. This is called braiding. The islands that you can see in the river at the bottom of Photo 1.3 are called chars. People sometimes choose to live on these islands.

a What are the chars made of?

b Why do you think some people choose to live on the chars?

c Why do you think it could be dangerous living on the chars?

d Draw a sketch of this part of Photo 1.3 to show the braiding of the rivers and the chars. Add labels to your sketch and give it a title.

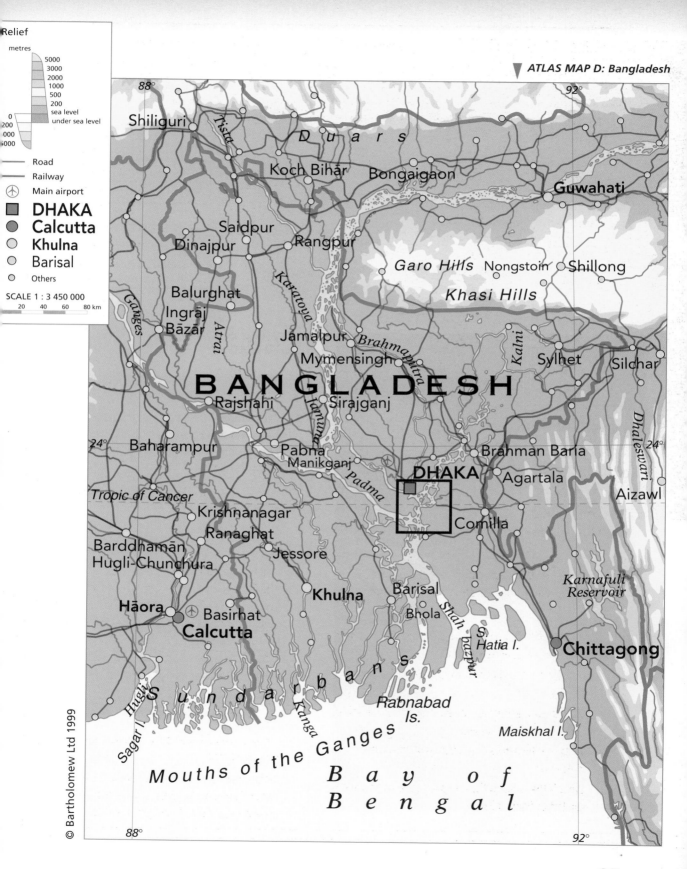

Relief

metres
- 5000
- 3000
- 2000
- 1000
- 500
- 200
- 0 sea level
- under sea level
- 200
- 000
- 4000

Road
Railway
Main airport

■ **DHAKA**
● **Calcutta**
○ Khulna
○ Barisal
∘ Others

SCALE 1 : 3 450 000

20 40 60 80 km

ATLAS MAP D: Bangladesh

88°   92°

Shiliguri

Tista

D u a r s

Koch Bihār   Bongaigaon   **Guwahati**

Saidpur
Dinajpur   Rangpur

Garo Hills Nongstoin ○ Shillong

Balurghat   *Khasi Hills*
Ingrāj
Bāzār
Ganges *Atrai* *Karatoya*   Jamalpur *Brahmaputra*   *Kalni* Sylhet   Silchar
Mymensingh

B A N G L A D E S H

Rajshahi   Sirajganj   *Dhaleswari*

24°   24°
Baharampur   Pabna   Brahman Baria
Manikganj   **DHAKA** Agartala
Tropic of Cancer   *Padma*   ■   Aizawl
Krishnanagar
Ranaghat   Comilla
Barddhamān   Jessore
Hugli-Chunchura   *Karnafuli*
                                                            Reservoir
Hāora   **Khulna**   Barisal
⊕ Basirhat   Bhola *Shah bazpur*
Calcutta   *S. Hatia I.* **Chittagong**

Hugli *S u n d a r b a n s* *Kanga* Rabnabad
Sagar I.   Is.   *Maiskhal I.*

Mouths of the Ganges   **B a y   o f**

B e n g a l

88°   92°

2 Population characteristics

Population growth

Between 1941 and 1998 the population of Bangladesh grew rapidly (Table 2.1). This was due to there being a high birth rate and a decreasing death rate.

There were several reasons why the birth rate was high in Bangladesh:

- large families meant that children could help in the fields or work to earn money

- children could support their parents in old age

- the infant death rate was high so parents felt that they needed to have many children in order that some would survive

- little contraception was available

2.1 Population growth in Bangladesh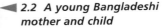

Year	Population in millions
1901	28
1941	42
1961	67
1974	76
1981	90
1991	111
1998	123

◄ 2.2 A young Bangladeshi mother and child

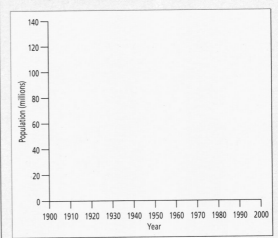

1 Study Table 2.1.

a Make a copy of the graph axes in Figure 2.3 and plot the data as a line graph to show the growth of Bangladesh's population.

▲ 2.3 Graph showing the growth of population in Bangladesh

b Use your graph to predict the population of Bangladesh for the years 2001 and 2021.

c Why has the growth rate begun to slow down in recent years?

2.4 A population pyramid for a ► typical economically developing country

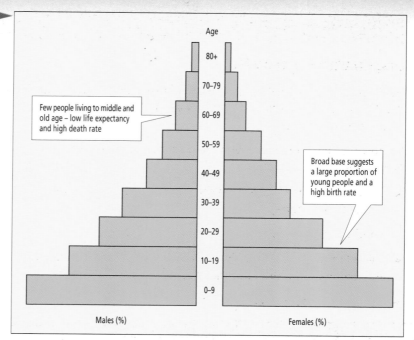

Few people living to middle and old age – low life expectancy and high death rate

Broad base suggests a large proportion of young people and a high birth rate

Males (%)   Females (%)

The death rate fell because new medicines and vaccinations were introduced. Infant deaths decreased dramatically so that families became very large.

The growth of Bangladesh's population has slowed down now. Parents know that infants are more likely to survive, so they have fewer children. In addition, there has been a successful family planning campaign. Nearly 50% of married women now use contraceptives, compared to less than 20% in 1981.

There is still much to do. In particular, women need to become more highly valued. They need to be given the chance to have a proper education and to follow a career. If marriage can be encouraged to take place later in life fewer children will be born.

Population structure

In an economically developing country such as Bangladesh, the majority of the population are very young. This is because the high birth rate results in many children being born. Typically there are not very many people living to old age. This is because diseases are more common and health care is less readily available.

To show the characteristics of a country's population structure a diagram called a **population pyramid** can be drawn (see Figure 2.4). Why do you think the diagram is called a 'pyramid'?

Population pyramids are useful to the government because they can be used to plan for the future. For example, if there is a very large number of young children, primary school places will need to be provided in the very near future.

2 Use the data in Table 2.5 to complete the population pyramid for Bangladesh.

▼ **2.5 Population structure in Bangladesh**

Age	Percentage of total population	
	Male	Female
70+	1%	1%
60–69	1%	1%
50–59	3%	2%
40–49	4%	3%
30–39	6%	5%
20–29	9%	8%
10–19	12%	12%
0–9	16%	16%

(Source: Population Concern)

a Add the following labels in their correct places:
 • large number of young people indicating a high birth rate
 • few people living to old age

3 How can a population pyramid help a government to plan for the future? (Hint: think about schools, health care for the elderly, housing, etc)

Population distribution

Bangladesh is one of the most densely populated countries in the world. However, because the country is mostly low-lying and fertile, and most of the population (82%) still live in the countryside, population is relatively evenly spread (see Figure 2.6).

The highest densities are found in the main cities and particularly around Dhaka, the capital. Notice that there are only two pockets of relatively low density.

Urbanisation

Only 16% of the population of Bangladesh live in towns and cities. The largest city is the capital Dhaka which has a

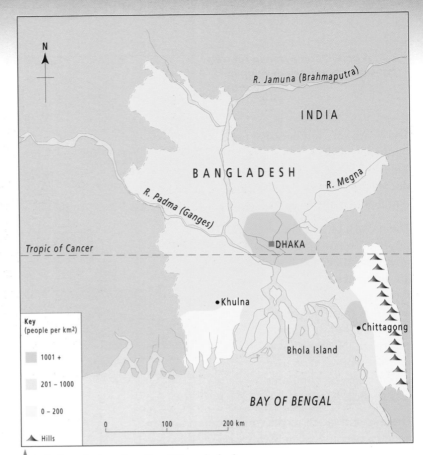

2.6 Population density of Bangladesh

2.7 Reasons given for migration to Dhaka

57% Economic reasons (for example, landless poverty, unemployment, getting charity)

25% Environmental causes (river bank erosion)

9% Personal or family reasons (loss of husband, dependants, family feud)

1% Socio-political reasons (social factors, village politics, brought by relatives)

8% Other reasons

population of about 9 million. Bangladesh's second city is Chittagong (see Atlas Map D page 95) which has just over 2 million people.

Cities, especially Dhaka, are growing rapidly mainly due to migration from the countryside. Look at Figure 2.7 to discover why people are moving to the city.

---

4 Make a careful copy of Figure 2.6 on a blank outline of Bangladesh.

a Use Atlas Map D (page 95) to label the following :
- Dhaka (high density)
- Chittagong (high density)
- Sundarbans (low density)
- hills east of Chittagong (low density)

b Why is the population fairly evenly distributed in Bangladesh?

c Why is there a pocket of low density in the Sundarbans area?

d Suggest reasons why the hills to the east of Chittagong also have a low population density.

---

5 Study Figure 2.7.

a Present the information as a bar graph or a pie chart. Use a colour key to explain each of the reasons given for migration to Dhaka.

b Are most of the reasons 'push' factors or 'pull' factors? Why do you think this is so?

c With reference to Photo 2.8, describe some of the conditions that newcomers might have to cope with on their arrival in Dhaka.

d Do you think the government's plan to reduce migration is a good idea? Explain your answer.

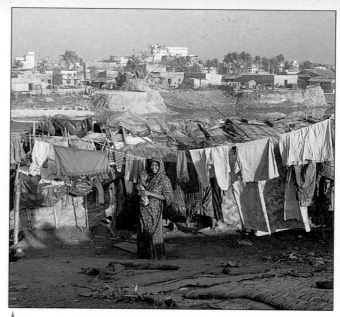

▲ *2.8 Bustees in Dhaka*

In common with other rapidly growing cities throughout the world, Dhaka is struggling to cope with the influx of newcomers. There are not enough houses, so shanty towns (called **bustees**) have grown up, where living conditions are generally poor (Photo 2.8). The city does not have enough jobs to go around and some people are forced to beg in order to survive.

Not everyone in Dhaka is poor. There are some who are wealthy and able to afford cars, private schools for their children and satellite television.

In an attempt to reduce the scale of migration, the government has invested in the many smaller towns throughout Bangladesh, building schools and hospitals in the hope that people will no longer feel the need to move to Dhaka.

3 Water, water, everywhere...

The flood of 1998

In 1998 severe flooding killed over 1,000 people and led to 23 million people becoming homeless. About two-thirds of the country was under water and rivers burst their banks. Over 125,000 cattle drowned, and vast areas of cropland were destroyed. The country's entire annual stock of rice was also destroyed. The city of Dhaka was virtually cut off by the floods – some two-thirds of the city became a vast pool of water, forcing people to travel along the city's streets by boat. People's lives were a misery both during, and for several months after, the flood (Figure 3.3).

▲ *3.1 Dhaka under water*

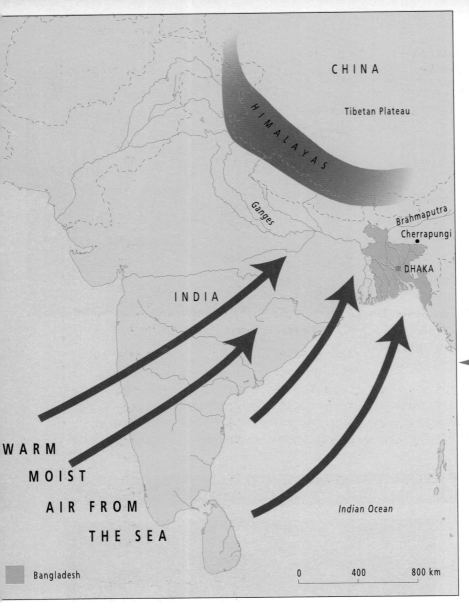

3.2 The summer monsoon

3.3 The 1998 monsoon tragedy

'Bangladesh's floods are killing people through drowning, electrocution and most dreaded of all, snake bites.'

'The lack of safe drinking water is causing diarrhoea. Prolonged exposure to germs in floodwater is causing skin diseases. But the number dying is relatively small for such a disaster-prone country. For most, the flood is a nuisance.'

'To shop for food you must wade, or wait for the metal packing-case ferry. To find safe drinking water you must lug your metal jars hundreds of metres to the nearest hand pump still in use. The gas supply is cut off or unreliable.'

'After the flood is gone, conditions will get even worse. The streets will be thick with vile mud, flies and other disease-carrying insects which will multiply and infections will become rampant.'

(Source: based on 'Monsoons pour tragedy on Bangladesh' Independent 7/9/98)

What causes floods in Bangladesh?

The 1998 flood was the result of the very heavy monsoonal rain that falls between June and October each year.

The **monsoon** is an important feature of the climate in Bangladesh and South Asia. In the summer, the continent of Asia becomes very hot. This causes the air to rise and, as it does so, it draws in warm and very moist air from the Indian Ocean to the south-west (see Figure 3.2). It is this air that produces the heavy monsoonal rain.

Much of the rain that causes flooding in Bangladesh actually falls in India. Look at Figure 3.2 to see how the Ganges and Brahmaputra rivers carry water into Bangladesh from neighbouring India.

3 Study Figure 3.2.

a Describe, with the help of a simple sketch map, the causes of the heavy monsoonal rain that led to the floods of 1998.

b How is it that Bangladesh suffers from another country's rain?

c Look back to the section about hurricanes on page 24. Write a few sentences suggesting why the coast of Bangladesh is at risk from floods caused by tropical cyclones (hurricanes).

4 Study Table 3.4.

a Draw a bar graph to show the Dhaka data in Table 3.4.

b Use a label to identify the monsoon period on your graph.

c What is the average annual rainfall in Dhaka?

d What proportion (fraction or percentage) of the total rainfall of Dhaka falls during the monsoon period?

5 Locate Cherrapungi on Figure 3.2. It is one of the wettest places in the world (see Table 3.5).

a What is the average annual rainfall of Cherrapungi? How does it compare to that of Dhaka?

b In June, there is over 2.6 metres of rain. How does this compare to your height?

c Using Figure 3.2, work out roughly where Cherrapungi is on Atlas Map D (it is not marked). How does its location help to explain the incredibly high amount of rain that falls there?

d Use Atlas Map D (page 95) to explain how the rainfall in the Cherrapungi area may cause problems for Bangladesh.

3.4 Average monthly rainfall for Dhaka, Bangladesh ▼

Month	Rainfall in mm
Jan	18
Feb	31
Mar	58
Apr	103
May	194
Jun	321
Jul	437
Aug	305
Sep	254
Oct	169
Nov	28
Dec	2

3.5 Average monthly rainfall for Cherrapungi, India ▼

Month	Rainfall in mm
Jan	18
Feb	53
Mar	185
Apr	666
May	1280
Jun	2695
Jul	2446
Aug	1781
Sep	1100
Oct	493
Nov	69
Dec	13

(Source: The World Weather Guide E.A. Pearce Hutchinson 1990)

As the swollen rivers slowly meander their way across the flat Bangladeshi landscape they frequently burst their banks, flooding the low-lying farmland. With the rivers so full, heavy rain in Bangladesh itself often remains ponded-up, unable to seep into the river channels.

Bangladesh is also hit by tropical cyclones (hurricanes) which bring heavy rain, storm surges and strong winds, particularly to the coastal fringe. In 1991, 139,000 people were killed in one of Bangladesh's worst cyclone disasters.

The benefits of flooding

Flooding is not always bad news. In fact, floods bring enormous benefits to the people of Bangladesh. The fertile silty soils that cover much of the country result from many years of flooding. Each flood deposits a new layer of fertile river sediment called **alluvium**. In addition, floodwater helps to irrigate crops. It is essential for the cultivation of rice, on which the whole population depends. Seasonally flooded land provides fish, an important source of protein for rural dwellers (Photo 3.6).

▲ *3.6 Flooding does bring some unexpected benefits. These boys are fishing in the floodwaters*

How can the dangers of flooding be reduced?

It is impossible to stop flooding in Bangladesh and, of course, it is in the interests of many that flooding continues. The Bangladesh Flood Action Plan aims to control rather than prevent flooding. Many kilometres of **embankments** have been built (Photo 3.7) to help protect towns and cities and to reduce the likelihood of rivers bursting their banks. At the same time, sluices have been built to enable farmers to draw water as they need it.

At the coast, **cyclone shelters** (Photo 3.9) have been built to house people evacuated from their homes. Built on 4-metre stilts, these shelters have been extremely successful in reducing the death toll from tropical cyclones.

▼ *3.7 Part of the flood embankment which surrounds Dhaka*

▲ **3.8 Sketch cross-section through an embankment near Dhaka**

3.9 Pekua cyclone shelter, Cox's Bazaar in south-east Bangladesh ▶

6 Study Photo 3.7.

a Make a copy of the sketch cross section in Figure 3.8.

b Add the following labels in their correct places to your sketch:
- flat, fertile farmland behind the embankment
- boats transporting produce and materials
- the embankment
- road on top of the embankment
- river

c Describe the purpose of flood embankments.

7 Floods are not always bad news for the people of Bangladesh. Describe some of the benefits of flooding, particularly for those who live in the countryside.

8 Study Photo 3.9.

a What is a cyclone shelter?

b Make a sketch of the cyclone shelter in Photo 3.9. Add labels to describe some of its features.

c Cyclone shelters have other uses for local communities. Can you suggest how else people might make use of them?

4 Bhola Island – living in the countryside

Bhola Island is one of the many islands that have formed where the three great rivers of Bangladesh, the Ganges (Padma), Brahmaputra (Jamuna) and Meghna, flow into the Bay of Bengal (Figure 4.1). Find Bhola Island on Atlas Map D (page 95). Notice that it is the largest island in Bangladesh.

Bhola Island is about 90 km in length and 20 km wide. The island is very flat – much of it is less than 1 metre above sea level. For this reason, and given the number of storms that hit the area, the whole island is encircled by a 7-metre high embankment. Despite the embankment, it still suffers regularly from flooding.

The Hawlader family

The Hawlader family (see Photo 4.2) live in the coastal village of Laximpur (see Figure 4.1). Forty-year-old Abul Kashim is the father of the family and he is married to Nojupha who is 32. They have five children aged between 14 and 5. The three youngest children, Shahinoor, Rohima and Shophizul appear in Photo 4.2 with their parents.

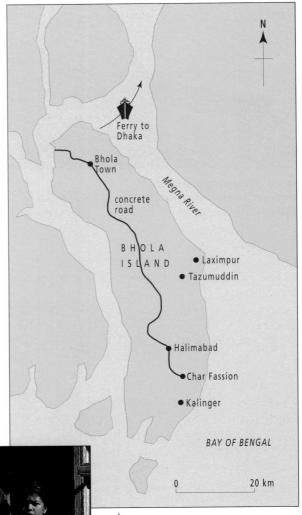

4.1 Bhola Island

4.2 The Hawlader family

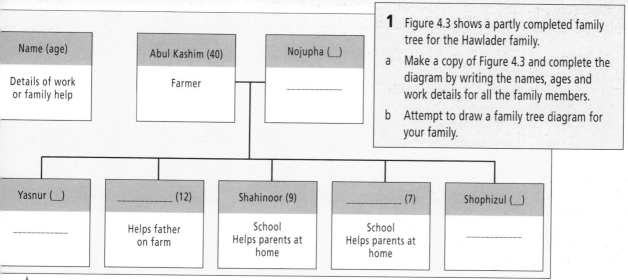

Name (age)	Abul Kashim (40)	Nojupha (__)
Details of work or family help	Farmer	_____

1 Figure 4.3 shows a partly completed family tree for the Hawlader family.

a Make a copy of Figure 4.3 and complete the diagram by writing the names, ages and work details for all the family members.

b Attempt to draw a family tree diagram for your family.

Yasnur (__)	_____ (12)	Shahinoor (9)	_____ (7)	Shophizul (__)
_____	Helps father on farm	School Helps parents at home	School Helps parents at home	_____

▲ *4.3 The Hawlader family tree*

In Photo 4.2 the family are standing in front of their house which is made of timber and corrugated-iron sheets. Behind the house is a kitchen made of bamboo and thatch and there is a pond which is used for bathing and washing clothes and dishes.

Abul Kashim is a farmer. He grows rice, potatoes, corn, onions and groundnuts (peanuts). Sometimes he earns extra money by mending fishing nets. Nojupha looks after the house, the children and the family's animals. She helps mend fishing nets, and dries and cleans the rice after it has been harvested. The eldest daughter, Yasnur, helps her mother with the household chores and is responsible for looking after the chickens. The eldest boy, Rofijul, helps his father on the farm and looks after the cattle. The three youngest children go to school but help their parents when they are at home.

Rice farming on Bhola Island

Rice is the staple food crop for most people living in south-east Asia. Most people grow their own, mainly to feed themselves and their families. This type of farming is called **subsistence** farming. It differs from **commercial** farming where crops are grown or livestock are kept in order to be sold.

Bangladesh's warm and wet climate is ideal for rice cultivation. Conditions are so good that it is possible for Abul Kashim to grow two crops of rice each year.

The farming year starts in June when the land is ploughed ready for the main rice crop. The rice seeds are planted in one corner of the field in early July just as the monsoon rains begin. Soon the young seedlings can be transplanted to mature in the ploughed field. Planting is done by hand: it is back-breaking work!

4.4 Abdul Kashim examining mature rice to see if it's ready to be harvested ▼

As the seedlings grow, Abul Kashim adds fertiliser to the soil and removes the weeds. After three months, shoots appear and a few weeks later the grains of rice are ripe and ready to harvest (Photo 4.4). Abul Kashim then cuts down the plants with a scythe and Nojupha dries them and removes the grains. Whilst most of the rice is used to feed the family some is sold at the local market.

In late December, the other crops (potatoes, corn, onions and groundnuts) are sown, as is the second rice crop. They grow during January and February and are harvested from March through to May.

Water supply on Bhola Island

Despite the heavy monsoon rains and the frequent flooding, the supply of safe water has been a real challenge to the people of Bhola Island. Much of the water held in tanks and in ponds and rivers is contaminated, and disease can spread rapidly if this water is used for drinking.

Safe water is obtained using **tube wells** that are sunk some 275 metres into the ground to tap underground water supplies. Once a hole has been sunk, a thin rubber tube is dropped into the well and attached to a pump at the top. A concrete slab holds the tube and the pump in place (Photo 4.6). Water can then be drawn up by moving the handle of the pump up and down.

A tube well is expected to provide safe water for up to 50 years. It is a vital first step in helping improve the quality of life for poor people. For this reason, aid agencies are often involved in helping to raise funds to sink tube wells. For example, Actionaid has constructed over 1,200 tube wells on Bhola Island, to bring safe water to over 250,000 people.

2 Farming types can be split into subsistence and commercial.

a Explain the difference between subsistence farming and commercial farming.

b Rice farming in Bangladesh is an example of subsistence farming. Make a list of ten examples of commercial farming. Try to include a good range of examples and see if you can include some that others in your class will not have thought of.

c Is Abul Kashim a subsistence or commercial farmer? Explain your answer.

▲ *4.5 Abul Kashim's farming year*

3 Figure 4.5 shows part of Abul Kashim's farming year.

a Make a copy of the diagram.

b Using the text, write captions for the pictures (1–4)..

c Now complete the yearly cycle by drawing pictures and adding captions for 5, 6, and 7.

4 In Book 2 you learned about the farming system. There are inputs, such as the climatic characteristics, workers and seeds, processes such as ploughing, and outputs such as wheat and milk. Make a list of the inputs, processes and outputs for Abul Kashim's farm. Present your information in the form of a flow diagram if you wish.

▲ *4.6 Rohima helping her mother to collect water*

4.7 A tube well ▶

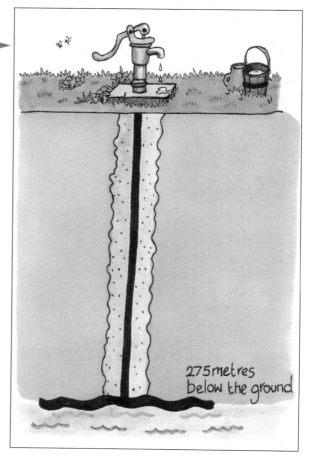

275 metres below the ground

5 Figure 4.7 shows the workings of the tube well shown in Photo 4.6.

a Make a copy of Figure 4.7 and add the following labels:
- concrete slab to hold the pump in place
- safe water, deep underground
- pump handle
- ground surface
- well sunk deep into the ground
- thin rubber tube

b Why have tube wells been sunk on Bhola Island?

6 Aid agencies such as Actionaid believe strongly in providing basic services for poor people such as tube wells. Why is the provision of safe water such a basic requirement if people's quality of life is to be improved?

The United States of America

The United States of America (the USA) is one of the most important and powerful countries in the world. It is one of the world's richest countries and most of its people enjoy a high standard of living.

1 The USA: an introduction

The USA is the fourth largest country in area in the world after Russia, Canada and China. It is part of the continent of North America and is made up of 50 states, including Alaska (north-west of Canada) and the islands of Hawaii far out in the Pacific Ocean (Figure 1.1).

CO	CONNECTICUT
M	MARYLAND
MASS	MASSACHUSETTS
RI	RHODE ISLAND
WV	WEST VIRGINIA

1.1 The USA and its states

ATLAS MAP E: North America

Russian Federation

Greenland

Iceland

Faeroes

U.S.A.

St Lawrence I.

Nunivak I.

Bering Strait

Pt Barrow

BEAUFORT SEA

Brooks Range

Yukon

Banks Island

Victoria Island

Queen Elizabeth Islands

Ellesmere Island

Parry Islands

BAFFIN BAY

Baffin Island

Davis Strait

Denmark Strait

Arctic Circle

Cape Farewell

Bristol Bay

Alaska Pen.

Kodiak I.

GULF OF ALASKA

Alaska Range

Mt McKinley 6194

Mt Logan 6050

Alexander Archipelago

CANADA

Queen Charlotte Islands

Coast Mountains

Mackenzie Mts

Great Bear

Great Slave L.

Peace

Mackenzie

Great Slave L.

Foxe Basin

Southampton

Hudson Strait

Labrador Sea

Belcher Is.

HUDSON BAY

Labrador

Newfoundland

Gulf of St Lawrence

Cape Breton I.

Vancouver Island

Fraser

ROCKY

GREAT PLAINS

Lake Athabasca

Churchill

Nelson

Severn

Lake Winnipeg

CANADIAN SHIELD

PACIFIC OCEAN

Seattle

Cascade Ra.

Columbia

MOUNTAINS

Yellowstone

Snake

Gannett Pk 4202

Missouri

Lake Superior

L. Huron

Detroit

Lake Michigan

Chicago

L. Erie

L. Ontario

St. Lawrence

Boston

C. Cod

New York

C. Sable

ATLANTIC OCEAN

U.S.A.

San Francisco

Sierra Nevada

Great Salt L.

Great Basin

Mt Whitney 4418

Colorado

Grand Canyon

Colorado Plateau

Arkansas

Ozark Plateau

Red

Ohio

Mississippi

Appalachian Mts

Washington

Chesapeake B.

C. Hatteras

Bermuda

Los Angeles

Phoenix

Rio Grande

Edwards Plateau

Dallas

C. Fear

Guadalupe

Gulf of California

Lower California

Sierra Madre Occidental

Altiplano Mexicano

Sierra Madre Oriental

New Orleans

C. Canaveral

Miami

Bahamas

Tropic of Cancer

GULF OF MEXICO

Str. of Florida

Cuba

Greater Antilles

Hispaniola

Puerto Rico

C. San Lucas

I. Clarión

MEXICO

Campeche Bay

Popocatépetl 5452

Sierra Madre del Sur

Yucatán

Yucatán Channel

G. of Honduras

Jamaica

CARIBBEAN SEA

Curaçao

Relief

Relief metres	
5000	
3000	
2000	
1000	
500	
200	
0	sea level
200	under sea level
4000	
6000	

Ice cap

SCALE 1 : 41 625 000

0   250   500   750   1000 km

© Bartholomew Ltd 1999

▲ *1.2a) Alaska*

▼ *1.2b) South Californian desert*

Contrasts in the USA

Given its size, it is hardly surprising that the USA has great geographical contrasts. Look at Photos 1.2a) and 1.2b) to see some of the contrasts in the landscape of the USA.

1 Relief. Look at Atlas Map E on page 109. Notice that much of western USA is mountainous. This chain of mountains, often referred to as the Rockies, stretches all the way from Alaska, through Canada and the USA, and into Central America. It then joins up with the Andes mountains that run down the western side of South America. Now look to the eastern side of the USA and locate another much smaller mountain range called the Appalachians.

Much of the rest of the USA consists of plains and lowlands, such as the Great Plains to the east of the Rockies, and the river deltas on the northern shores of the Gulf of Mexico.

2 Climate. The USA has a huge variety of climates. This is because it extends over a large range of latitudes from Hawaii in the hot tropics to Alaska in the cold sub-Arctic. Look back to Chapter 2 to find the range of climates in the USA.

Being a large continental land mass, much of inland USA has a continental climate. This means that it has great extremes of temperature with very hot summers and cold winters. The reason for such extremes is because land heats up and cools down much more quickly than water. The climates of coastal regions or islands, such as the UK, are far less extreme as temperatures are greatly moderated by the sea. Rainfall also tends to be less in continental interiors because it is far from the sea. You might remember learning about this in Book 2.

3 People. About 75% of the population of the USA live in towns and cities. This compares to only 16% in Bangladesh. Within the cities, as in Bangladesh, there are huge contrasts between the poor and the rich (see Photos 1.3a) and 1.3b)). Large numbers of people have migrated to the United States from abroad in search of work. Today there are particularly large numbers of people originating from Africa (descendants of the slaves brought in by the British), Central Mexico and the Caribbean, Western Europe and Asia.

1.3a) A poor area of New York

1.3b) A rich area of New York

THE UNITED STATES OF AMERICA

1 In this activity you will be drawing a map to show some of the main characteristics of the geography of the USA. You will need a blank outline map of North America.

a Use a pencil to carefully draw the lines of latitude and longitude. They will help you locate the other geographical features listed below.

b Using a pencil, draw on to your map the mountains, the rivers and the location of the cities shown on Figure 1.4 . Draw the borders of the USA too. Do not do any writing yet.

c Use the following colours to make these features stand out more clearly:
- mountains: brown
- rivers: blue
- cities : black
- USA borders: red

d Refer to Atlas Map E (page 109) and use ink to label the following:
- **Mountains**
  Rocky Mountains
  Appalachians
  Alaska Range
  Sierra Nevada
  Cascades
  Mt McKinley
- **Rivers and lakes**
  Mississippi   Missouri
  Ohio   Yukon
  St Lawrence   Rio Grande
  Colorado   Snake
  Lake Superior   Lake Michigan
- **Physical regions**
  Mississippi delta
  Great Plains   Great Basin
- **Sea areas**
  Atlantic Ocean
  Pacific Ocean
  Gulf of Mexico
  Gulf of California
  Gulf of Alaska
- the degrees of latitude and longitude

e Now use ink to add the cities as shown on Figure 1.4, or write them in a key.

f Label Canada, Mexico, the USA and the state of Alaska.

g Complete your map by adding a key, a scale, a north point and a title.

2 In this activity you will be drawing a map to show the climate of the USA. You will need a blank map outline of North America. Turn back to the world climate map on page 22.

a Using a pencil, draw the climate regions on to your map.

b Use colours to shade each climate type and explain them in a key.

c Complete your map by writing a title.

d Write a few sentences describing the variety of climates in the USA. Use your map completed in Activity 1 to enable you to refer to places or regions.

1.4 The basic geography of the USA ▼

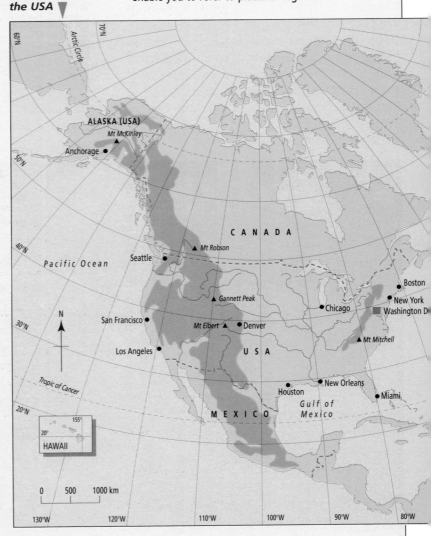

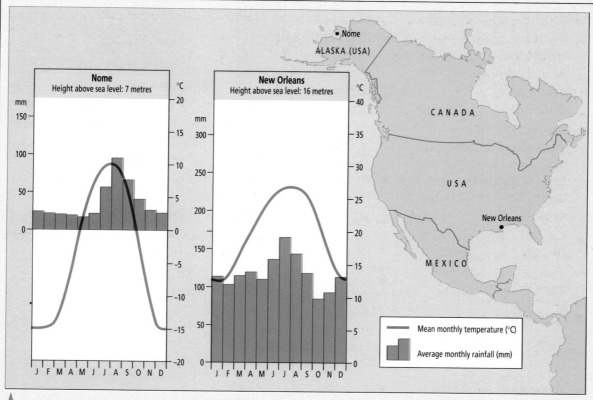

▲ *1.5 Climate graphs for Nome and New Orleans*

3 Study the climate graphs for New Orleans and Nome in Figure 1.5. Write a short account comparing the two climates represented by these two places. To do this, you should do the following :

Step 1

Note down as many differences and similarities as you can between the two climate graphs. Here are some questions you should try to answer.

- In which month is the highest rainfall? How much is it?
- What is the average annual rainfall?
- Does rain fall throughout the year or is it concentrated in certain seasons? (In Nome, some of the winter 'rain' will be in the form of snow!)
- What are the highest and lowest mean monthly temperatures and when are they recorded?
- How do temperatures vary throughout the year?

Step 2

- Think about how you are going to organise your written comparison.
- What order are you going to write things? Make a rough plan.

Step 3

- Write your account.
- Make sure that you compare New Orleans and Nome throughout your account – do not write separate paragraphs on each place.
- Include sketches of the climate graphs if you wish.
- Try to suggest some reasons for the differences.
- How do you think the climates affect people's everyday lives?

This is your own account so **you** decide what to do and how to do it!

4 Use the information in this unit (see page 114 too) to produce a poster describing the geography of the USA. Include a mixture of writing and illustrations (maps, diagrams and sketches) and take some time to plan the layout of your poster before starting.

Further information about the USA can be found in atlases, encyclopedias (including CD-ROMs such as Encarta) and on the Internet.

THE UNITED STATES OF AMERICA

▼ 1.7 Factfile: USA

- The USA has a population of 269 million people which is far more than the UK (58 million) or Bangladesh (123 million).

- The USA has an area of 9,372,000 sq km which is far greater than that of the UK (244,000 sq km) or Bangladesh (144,000 sq km).

- There are many natural resources including oil, coal, iron, bauxite, gold and uranium.

- The USA is the world's largest emitter of the 'greenhouse' gas carbon dioxide.

- There are many natural hazards that threaten the USA including hurricanes, tornadoes, volcanoes, earthquakes, floods and wildfires.

- The USA became independent from England on 4 July 1776.

- There are over 6 million km of roads in the USA.

- 93% of Americans do not own a passport.

- 34,000 people are killed by guns every year.

- There are over 193 million television sets in private use.

- Washington DC was established as the capital city in 1790. It is home to the seat of government and to the White House, the President's residence.

- Hollywood in Los Angeles is the centre of the world's film industry.

Web search

Up-to-date information about the USA can be found in the CIA's World Factbook at http:// www.odci.gov/cia/publications/factbook/us.html

Land use	
arable crops	20%
meadows and pasture	26%
forest/woodland	29%
others	25%
TOTAL	100%

Labour force	
managerial, professional	27%
technical, sales, managerial support	31%
services	14%
manufacturing, mining, transport, crafts	25%
farming, forestry, fishing	3%
TOTAL	100%

2 San Francisco, California

The view of San Francisco from the Golden Gate Bridge (Photo 2.1) is a famous one. With a population of over 2 million people, San Francisco is one of America's largest cities. It is a wealthy city with many gleaming, modern tower blocks including the distinctive Transamerica Pyramid. Can you spot this building in Photo 2.1?

San Francisco is sited on a peninsula of land that juts northwards to form the southern entrance to San Francisco Bay (see Figure 2.2). The city is part of a vast horseshoe-shaped urban area known as the San Francisco Bay Area. The Bay Area contains other important cities such as San

Jose, which is close to the world famous computer centre called 'Silicon Valley'. In addition to the high technology industry, the San Francisco Bay Area has many other thriving industries such as retailing, banking, and biomedical research.

San Francisco sits on one of the most active plate margins in the world, the San Andreas Fault. Earthquakes frequently rock the city and, in 1906, much of the city was destroyed by fire following a powerful earthquake.

The growth of San Francisco

San Francisco started life as a small sleepy seaport concentrating mainly on the export of cattle hides. Gold was discovered nearby and the great Californian Gold Rush started in the mid-1800s, with thousands of hopeful prospectors migrating from the east in search of wealth. The city grew rapidly into a bustling and very wealthy outpost.

Today it is regarded as one of America's leading business and financial centres and it has important links with countries of the Pacific Rim, such as South Korea.

For many years San Francisco has attracted artists and free-thinkers. It is a tolerant city with a very diverse population and people from many different races and backgrounds. It is a popular tourist destination.

1 Look at the information about San Francisco and answer the following questions:

a With the help of a simple sketch map, describe the site of San Francisco.

b Why do you think the site was chosen for an early settlement?

c Why did San Francisco suddenly begin to grow in the mid-1800s?

d What is the name of the large urban sprawl of which San Francisco is a part?

▼ *2.1 San Francisco from the Golden Gate Bridge*

▼ *2.2 Satellite image of San Francisco Bay Area*

2 The satellite image (Figure 2.2) uses a range of colours to show different land uses in the San Francisco Bay Area. The colours are generated by a computer, and satellite images of this kind are called false colour images, for obvious reasons! Can you identify the colours used to show:
- woodland
- built-up area
- water

3 Draw a sketch map of the San Francisco Bay Area. Remember to use a pencil first before using colours. Write your labels in ink at the end of the exercise.

a Use Atlas Map F to draw on the extent of the following land uses:

- built-up area
- marsh
- salt marsh

b Locate the following reservoirs:
- Crystal Springs Reservoirs
- San Andreas Lake
- Upper San Leando Reservoir
- Lake Chabot

c Draw on to your map the following bridges:
- Golden Gate
- Dumbarton Bridge
- San Francisco-Oakland Bay Bridge

d Locate these cities:
- San Francisco
- San Jose
- Hayward
- Oakland

e Label the Pacific Ocean and San Francisco Bay

f Complete your map by using colours and adding written labels for all the different features that you have plotted.

ATLAS MAP F: San Francisco Bay Area

KEY

Relief and physical features

metres
900
600
300
0

599 ▲ Mountain height (in metres)

River

Lake / Reservoir

Marsh

Salt marsh

Woodland

Communications

Railway

Motorway

Road

⊕ Main airport

Settlement

Built-up area

Cities and towns

◎ over 500 000 population

◉ 100 000 -500 000 population

○ under 100 000 population

SCALE 1:446 000

0   5   10   15 km

Place names and features

San Rafael, San Rafael Bay, Richmond-San Rafael Bridge, spur, Corte Madera, Mill Valley, Tiburon Peninsula, Tiburon, Marin Peninsula, Sausalito, Angel Island, Alcatraz Island, Golden Gate, San Francisco, Lake Merced, Daly City, Brisbane, South San Francisco, San Bruno, Pacifica, San Andreas Lake, Point San Pedro, Pedro Valley, Montara Mountain, Pilarcitos Lake, El Granada, Pillar Point, Half Moon Bay, Arroyo Leon

Richmond, El Cerrito, Albany, Brooks Island, Berkeley, Piedmont, Oakland, Alameda, San Pablo Reservoir, Redwood Cr., Upper San Leandro Reservoir, San Leandro, Lake Chabot, Oakland International Airport, San Lorenzo, Potrero Pt., San Francisco Bay, San Francisco International Airport, Coyote Pt., Foster City, Burlingame, San Mateo, San Mateo Cr., San Mateo Bridge, Redwood Pt., Greco Island, San Carlos, San Carlos Airport, Lower Crystal Springs Res., Upper Crystal Springs Res., Pilarcitos Cr., Redwood City, Menlo Park, Woodside, 641, Purisima Cr., Lobitos Cr., Tunitas Cr.

Briones Reservoir, Lafayette, Lafayette Reservoir, Orinda, Alamo, Walnut Creek, Danville, Sycamore Cr., Bollinger Cr., Black Hills, Mt. Diablo 1173, San Ramon, Dublin, Alamo Cr., Castro Valley, Hayward, Pleasanton Ridge, Sunol Ridge, Walpert Ridge, Union City, Alameda Cr., Fremont, Newark, Palo Alto, Stanford, Palo Alto Airport, Coyote Cr., Mountain View, Felt Lake, Sunnyvale, Cupertino, San Jose International Airport, Santa Clara, San Jose, Reid Hillview Airport, Campbell, Milpitas, U. Penitencia, Alum Rock, Berryessa Cr., Silver Cr., Coyote Cr., Calaveras Reservoir

Pacific Ocean, 668, Black Mtn. 838, Monte Bello Ridge, Stevens Cr., Stevens Cr. Reservoir, Saratoga, Mt. Bielawski 985, Butano Ridge, El Corte de Madera, Bogess Cr., La Honda Cr., Pescadero Cr., Pomponio Cr., Pescadero Point, Butano Cr., Bean Hollow Lake, Pigeon Point, Franklin Point, Whitehouse Cr., Gatos Cr., Mill Cr., Scott Cr., Waddell Cr., Año Nuevo Bay, 758, Boulder Creek, Loch Lomond, Ben Lomond, Felton, Scotts Valley, Boulder Cr., Los Gatos, Los Gatos Cr., Lexington Reservoir, Guadalupe Reservoir, Almaden Reservoir, Cambrian Park, Santa Teresa Hills, Alamitos Cr., SAN ANDREAS RIFT ZONE, Santa Cruz Mountains

The centre of San Francisco

Most cities in America have a similar and very distinctive street layout. Look at the street map of central San Francisco (Figure 2.5). Notice that the roads generally form a grid-square pattern. This is because San Francisco is a relatively modern planned city. It is quite different to many old world cities such as London with their haphazard street patterns reflecting a very long history and a lack of early planning.

Take time to study Figure 2.5. Notice the large number of piers indicating the importance of trade to the growth of the city. Can you find the University of San Francisco, Fisherman's Wharf, Chinatown and the Golden Gate Bridge?

▲ **2.4a)** *A view of Alcatraz Island, looking down Van Ness Avenue*

▲ **2.4b)** *Fisherman's Wharf*

▲ **2.5 San Francisco city centre**

0 METRES 1000
0 YARDS 1000

---

4 Study Figure 2.5.

a Locate the Sunset district and describe the street layout.

b Which two museums are located in Golden gate Park?

c Along which street would you travel between the Young Museum and the City Hall?

d Which museum is located next to Fisherman's Wharf?

e What major landmark is located on Columbus Avenue?

f What evidence is there that the land in the Twin Peaks district is hilly?

g Describe a main road route from the Golden Gate Bridge to the San Francisco-Oakland Bay Bridge.

5 Would you like to visit San Francisco? Explain your answer.

3 Cotton-growing in the Cotton Belt

If you look at the labels on the clothes that you are wearing you will probably find that they are made of cotton. Cotton is more widely used than any other fibre in making textiles, such as clothes, curtains, and furniture covers. Look at Figure 3.1 to discover what else cotton fibre is used to make.

What is cotton?

The fluffy cotton fibres that you can see in the photograph in Photo 3.2 are found in pods called **bolls**. They form from the flowers that blossom on the thorny bushes in the springtime in the same way that apples and other fruits are formed from flowering blossom.

Cotton is a commercial crop because it is grown to be sold. This type of crop is also called a **cash crop**. Look at Figure 3.1 and notice that it is not only the fibres that are a valuable product of cotton.

The United States produces 20% of the world's cotton. It is the U.S.'s most important cash crop and supplies a great many industries, supporting over 340,000 jobs.

▼ *3.1 What is cotton used for?*

Meal and hulls (remains of seeds after oil is extracted)

Animal Feed
Fish Feed
Fertiliser

Oil (from seeds)

cooking oil
Salad dressing
Margarine

Cotton fibre

clothing
curtains
Tents
Book Binding
Coffee filters

◀ *3.2 Fields of cotton plants*

1 Study Figure 3.1.

a Make a list of some items made from cotton in your home.

b Where does cotton oil come from and what is it used for?

c How can cotton meal and hulls be used to improve the condition of the soil?

d Make a copy of Figure 3.1.
  - Add your list of cotton items (Activity 1a)
  - Write a label to identify the bolls on the cotton plants

2 Study Table 3.3.

a Copy Table 3.3 and complete the columns. To do this, you need to follow the example given for Argentina.

b Use the values in the degrees column to construct a pie chart to show the main producers of cotton fibre in the world. Use different colours for each country and explain them in a key.

c Which is the only country to produce more cotton fibre than the United States?

d Which continent produces the bulk of the world's cotton fibre?

e One of the major importers of cotton fibre is the European Union. Can you explain why?

▼ **3.3 World production of cotton fibre (1995)**

Country	Production (thousand tonnes)	%	degrees
Argentina	402	2.03	7.3
Brazil	515		
China	4768		
Greece	420		
India	2380		
Pakistan	1835		
Turkey	755		
Turkmenistan	403		
USA	3912		
Uzbekistan	1306		
Rest of world	3103		
TOTAL	19799		

(Source : Philips Geographical Digest 1998-99)

To calculate the percentage of world production for Argentina

$$\frac{402}{19799} \times 100 = 2.03\%$$

To convert this percentage into degrees, multiply by 3.6

2.03 x 3.6 = 7.3 degrees

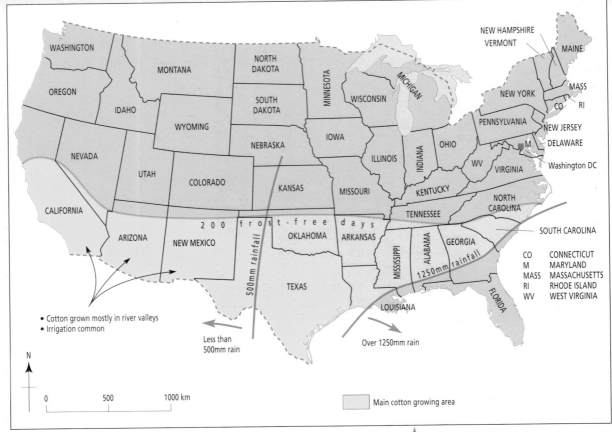

▲ **3.4 Cotton growing in the sunbelt**

Where is cotton grown?

Cotton production is concentrated in the southern United States in a broad zone known as the Cotton Belt (see Figure 3.4). Cotton grows best under the following conditions:

- more than 200 frost-free days a year to enable the plant to grow and mature fully

- an annual rainfall of over 500 mm (approximately the same as in London) but less than 1,250 mm

- reasonably fertile soils

Look at Figure 3.4 and notice that cotton is also grown to the west of the 500 mm minimum rainfall line where, in theory, conditions are too dry. The only way that cotton can be grown here is by using irrigation.

▲ **3.5 Harvesting cotton in the US**

Cotton was first produced commercially in the southern states such as Mississippi, Georgia and Alabama. Slaves were used widely to work on the huge cotton plantations until they were freed during the American Civil War in 1863. The plantations were then divided into smallholdings which turned out to be far less efficient than the plantations had been. Careless farming methods before and after the Civil War reduced the fertility of the soils and led to serious soil erosion. Production fell in these traditional areas and cotton growing spread eastwards into Texas and then on to California.

Today cotton production is largely controlled by the government. Each year the government tells farmers how many hectares of cotton can be grown. This is to prevent there being a surplus which could cause prices to fall and farmer's income to drop. The poorer, less efficient farmers in the original cotton growing areas of the south receive price supports from the government to stop them going out of business and becoming unemployed.

3 Draw a choropleth map to show the information in Table 3.6. For this activity you will need a blank map outline of the states of the USA.

▼ *3.6 Cotton production in the United States (1998)*

State	Production (bales)
Alabama	545
Arkansas	1150
Arizona	590
California	1250
Florida	83
Georgia	1500
Louisiana	670
Mississippi	1500
Missouri	390
New Mexico	96
North Carolina	927
Oklahoma	100
South Carolina	315
Tennessee	550
Texas	3000
Virginia	146

(Source : National Cotton Council of America)

a Use the following colour key to shade the states where cotton is grown:
1–499 bales   yellow
500–999 bales   orange
1000–1499 bales   red
1500+   brown

(A bale is a standard unit of cotton production, equivalent to about 230 kg.)

b Refer back to Figure 3.4 and draw the following climatic lines on to your map
● 200 frost-free days
● 500 mm annual rainfall
● 1250 mm annual rainfall

c Complete your map by adding a key and a title.

4 Study your map produced in Activity 3 and the writing earlier in this unit.
a Which state produces the most cotton?
b How important are climatic factors in controlling where cotton is grown?
c Why has production declined in the original cotton states?
d How can cotton be produced in the drier western states?
e In what ways does government action affect cotton farmers?

4 Enquiry: managing visitors in Yosemite Valley

The aim of this Enquiry is for you to make a study of the impact of visitors in Yosemite (pronounced "Yos-em-ittee") Valley and to examine how the valley should be managed in the future. In your report you should consider the following questions:

a Where is Yosemite Valley and what makes it attractive to visitors?

b What are the problems caused by visitors to the valley?

c How can the valley be managed in the future to meet the aims of the National Parks?

Study the information in this unit very carefully. Then either make up your own report plan or work through the following Activities.

Yosemite Valley is the most popular attraction in Yosemite National Park, California (Figure 4.1). There are 54 National Parks in the United States and, with 3.6 million visitors a year, Yosemite is one of the most popular.

There are two aims of the U.S. National Parks

● to protect the natural environment for future generations

● to allow visitors to gain access and enjoy the countryside

Increasingly, the vast numbers of visitors are having harmful effects on the natural environment and careful management is needed to protect the Parks for the future.

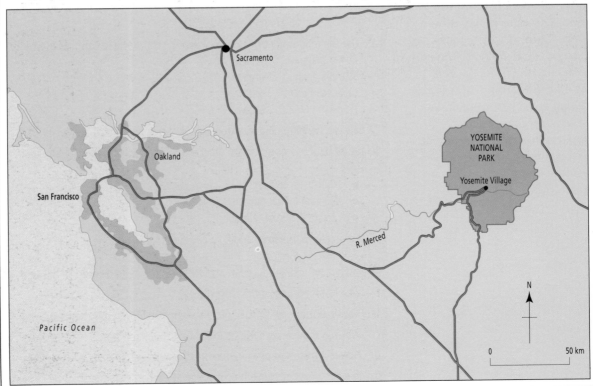

▼ **4.1 Location of Yosemite National Park. The valley, where nearly all the visitors go, is shown by the roads going to and from Yosemite Village**

ENQUIRY
A

The attractions of Yosemite Valley

A1 Half Dome ▲

A2 Yosemite Falls ▶

1 Draw a map to show the location of Yosemite National Park and Yosemite Valley.

2 Study the information in Photos A1 and A2 and make a list of the attractions for visitors to Yosemite Valley.

3 Study Figure 4.1

a How far is Yosemite National Park from
  ● San Francisco?
  ● Sacramento?

b What river runs through Yosemite National Park?

ENQUIRY B The problems caused by visitors to Yosemite Valley

B1 What problems are caused by visitors? ▼

Tourist traffic turning park into parking lot

Towering falls, ancient sequoias (trees) and the world's most famous sheer rock attract millions of visitors to this geological shrine. They arrive and find traffic gridlock, pine scent smothered by exhaust, sold out campgrounds and long queues to buy food, go to the bathroom (toilet), catch a shuttle bus or ride a horse.

On peak summer weekends in Yosemite Valley, the park's scenic heart, it's common to see rangers directing traffic and rows of tour buses idling at top attractions. Cars endlessly circle jammed parking lots, shuttles are full to standing room only, and the late-afternoon exodus is a bumper-to-bumper crawl.

Gabriela Tigges, on a two day visit with her three kids, said "Instead of being enjoyable, this trip has turned into torture. If the cars could be outside and we could be inside then we could be in tune with the park."

In the 1950s 1 million people visited the park each year. This figure rose to 2 million in the 1970s and topped 3 million for the first time in 1987. There is a growing concensus that, short of limiting visitors, the best solution to Yosemite's gridlock is to limit private vehicles.

Wear and tear shows up in the valley. Years ago, boardwalks had to be built through meadows to keep visitors from trampling them. Now the boardwalks have to be roped so people stay on them. River and creek banks have eroded from foot traffic wearing away vegetation.

(Source: USA Today August 3 1998)

1 Read the newspaper article (Figure B1) and identify the problems caused by visitors to the valley. Suggest how these problems might affect the future of the park.

▼ B2 Table of visitors to Yosemite 1997

Visitors to Yosemite National Park (1997)	
January	12,520
February	64,201
March	136,476
April	200,212
May	319,108
June	460,459
July	595,059
August	697,060
September	516,567
October	372,171
November	168,533
December	127,604

(Source: National Parks Service – Internet)

2 Present the information in Table B2 as a line graph to discover what time of year the park is under greatest pressure from visitors

ENQUIRY C

Managing visitors in Yosemite Valley

▼ **C1 Proposals for managing Yosemite Valley**

1 Reduce traffic congestion by a combination of actions:

a expanding the free shuttle service by using electric buses in addition to the diesel ones aleady in use

b construction of car parks outside the valley with buses bringing people in

c visitors use a reservation system to book entry into the park

2 Replace the campsites destroyed by the 1997 flood

3 Remove National Park maintenance and services (various buildings and machinery) from the valley and locate elsewhere

4 Improve services for visitors (e.g. toilets, food outlets)

5 Improve notices and information points to enable visitors to gain more from their visit

6 Removal of kerbside parking areas

7 Meadows restored and boardwalks constructed

(Source : Based on Draft Yosemite Valley Implementation Plan)

1 Study the list of management proposals in Figure C1. Suggest how each proposal might help to

● reduce the damage done by visitors

● improve the quality of visitors' experiences

2 In 1997 a devastating flood caused considerable damage in the valley. Read Figure C2 to discover what happened. What effect do you think this flood has had on future management of the valley?

3 How do you think Yosemite Valley should be managed? Remember that your ideas must deliver the aims of the National Parks.

▼ **C2 The Yosemite Valley flood of 1997**

In early January 1997 heavy rain and melting snow combined to create the greatest flood of the River Merced for over 80 years. Roads, bridges buildings and campsites were destroyed and an estimated $178 million of damage was caused.

Almost 300 guest lodging units at Yosemite Lodge were inundated by 2 metres of water and 250 units at Housekeeping Camp were flooded, leaving extensive sand and debris deposits. Over 900 camping pitches were destroyed with Lower and Upper River Campsites being particularly badly affected.

Earlier plans for the valley had argued for developments to be above the floodplain. In a matter of a few hours it became clear that these plans should have been followed.

(Source : Based on Yosemite National Park info. from the Internet)

INDEX